D1562516

REFLECTIONS ON THE SUNDAY READINGS

Reflections on the Sunday Readings

Preparing for the Liturgy of the Word,
Following the A, B, and C Cycles of the Lectionary

Richard T.A. Murphy, O.P.

Servant Publications
Ann Arbor, Michigan

Published by Servant Publications
P.O. Box 8617
Ann Arbor, Michigan 48107

Cover design by Michael Andaloro

91 92 93 94 95 10 9 8 7 6 5 4 3 2 1

Printed in the United States of America
ISBN 0-89283-633-4

Library of Congress Cataloging-in-Publication Data

Murphy, Richard Thomas Aquinas, 1908–
  Reflections on the Sunday readings / preparing for the liturgy of
the Word, following the A,B, and C cycles of the lectionary /
Richard T.A. Murphy.
      p.   cm.
  ISBN 0-89283-716-0
  1. Church year meditations.   2. Bible—Liturgical lessons.
3. Catholic Church—Prayer-books and devotions—English. I. Title.
BX2170.C55M87   1991
264'.34—dc20   91–27419

Contents

Acknowledgment

To David and Sue Mallaun, my sincere thanks for their considerable help in preparing this manuscript for publication. Their expertise in using computers is matched only by their willingness to use this new technology to help others.

Introduction

Have you ever found yourself rushing off to Sunday Mass and then leaving church unable to remember the readings and the homily? Or do you quickly forget the main theme of the readings and the homily once the work week begins?

If you fall into either of these two categories, you have plenty of company. The simple fact is many Catholics struggle to remember the Sunday readings and then apply the message to their daily lives.

In *Reflections on the Sunday Readings*, I have developed brief summary reflections that tie together the main theme of each Sunday's readings. I have also attempted to apply the message to some aspect of daily Christian life. It is my sincere hope that these reflections will help you remember and apply God's Word to your life.

The church looks upon God's Word as bread from heaven that nourishes the soul. Nourishment, however, does not automatically follow from mere contact with the Bible. One must ponder over and digest what is read or heard. Like the Virgin Mary, we too must live in faith and grow in the knowledge of God. May these reflections help you to ponder, digest, and be truly nourished by the Word of God.

> Let not the wise man glory in his wisdom
>   nor the strong man glory in his strength,
>   nor the rich man glory in his riches;
> But rather, let him who glories, glory in this,
>   that in his prudence he knows me,... **Jeremiah 9:22-23**

THE LECTIONARY

What are the Sunday readings based upon? The lectionary for Mass first appeared in 1971, replacing the one that had been used by the church since 1570. This is a *new* lectionary. Most significantly, it is the first time all the readings are now in the vernacular; we have a lectionary in English alone.

Another feature in the "reform" of the Liturgy, brought about by Vatican II, is that the readings come from a much wider selection of passages. Previously unheard portions of the Bible have been introduced for the first time. The faithful now have set before them a carefully prepared, lavish fare, rich and immensely satisfying.

In the course of the year, the main themes of the Bible are set before the faithful. Nothing of religious significance is overlooked. There is much about God's love and mercy, while also acknowledging the appropriateness at times of God's wrath, judgment, and punishment. Many passages which call for social action are balanced by others which stress the personal dimensions of holiness and union with God. We are shown a world that is passing and a world that is without end, a world of prophets and kings, of apostles and ordinary believers. All aspects of life are touched upon. The Bible thus enriches our minds and increases our devotion to the Lord.

The Paschal Mystery, of course, is the focal point of the new lectionary. It constitutes the great "mystery" predicted by the prophets, realized in Christ Jesus, and shared in by all who have been baptized and believe. The proclamation of the Word centers on this mystery.

HOW TO USE THIS BOOK

The new lectionary for Sunday Mass is easy to use. The readings basically follow the seasons of the church year: Advent, Christmas, Lent, Easter, and Ordinary Time.

The readings are organized into three sets or cycles, A, B, and C.

Each set is used in turn for a whole liturgical year. The following calendar identifies the liturgical cycles for the next thirteen years:

1990 A	1993 A	1996 A	1999 A	2002 A
1991 B	1994 B	1997 B	2000 B	2003 B
1992 C	1995 C	1998 C	2001 C	2004 C

Each liturgical year begins on the first Sunday of Advent and ends on the last Sunday of Ordinary Time ("Christ the King"). In this book, the Sunday readings are organized according to when they actually appear during the church year, instead of simply by season. Practically, this means there is a separate chapter for Sundays in Ordinary Time before the Lenten Season and one for those that fall after the Easter Season. The Scripture references for each Sunday's readings are listed above the reflection for the reader's convenience.

One final practical point: Holy Days of Obligation and major feasts of the Proper of Saints usually replace the Sunday Mass readings with those of their own when they fall on Sunday. However, there are only six instances of such a replacement over the next five years, so I have decided not to include a section of such supplanting feasts. For the reader's convenience, the six instances are listed below:

1. The Immaculate Conception, December 8, 1991
2. The Presentation, February 2, 1992
3. All Saints, November 1, 1992
4. The Assumption, August 15, 1993
5. St. Joseph, March 19, 1995
6. The Transfiguration, August 6, 1995

In these instances I recommend that you consult a Sunday missal or the lectionary to locate the appropriate readings.

In these pages, may you feast on the Word of God and find nourishment for your soul. May you recognize, Sunday after Sunday, how it applies to your life and seek to live the gospel.

Year A

Sunday Readings

ONE

Advent Season

HE IS COMING
First Sunday of Advent

1. Isaiah 2:1-5
2. Romans 13:11-14
3. Matthew 24:37-44

THE PASSING OF TIME regularly brings us to the season we call Advent. It is a time to look ahead, for Christmas will soon be here and we await its coming eagerly. Advent means "coming."

The mere mention of Christmas fills the mind with fond memories and expectation. Isaiah sang of the future glory of Zion, the city of God. We sing in praise of the Lord Jesus who has come and is to come to his city, the world, and into our hearts.

Isaiah envisioned peoples making their way to a holy mountain to learn about God and his wondrous kingdom of peace. There the weapons of war ("swords" and "spears") would be changed into instruments of peace. There justice and harmony would no longer be a dream but a glorious reality. Enmity and war would be no more.

The purple vestments worn at Mass today remind us that the royal personage who was to come and has come, is a King, and rules now in his kingdom, the church.

The world before Christ, though full of natural beauty, was nonetheless spiritually darkened. As St. Paul says, deeds of darkness flourish in the world. Light, however, as befits children of the Light, has come into the world through Christ. It is time now then to lead decent and honorable lives.

Paul knew the vices of the world, and named them: drunkenness, immorality, quarreling, and jealousy. Such vices must be fought against by Christian soldiers bearing the arms of prayer and virtue.

Jesus is always coming to us, and Advent helps us prepare for him. God's plan unfolds according to a time plan not revealed to us, and it behooves us always to be prepared for this great and joyful event. Advent is a time for prayer.

CHRIST, OUR LEADER
Second Sunday of Advent

1. Isaiah 11:1-10
2. Romans 15:4-9
3. Matthew 3:1-12

EVERY SOCIETY must have a leader. Fraternities, card-clubs, athletic teams, and corporations all have directors. Without a guiding hand things do not get done, and many worthy causes languish.

In religion too, there is need for a leader. His name is God. We have never seen him, but thanks to the prophets, we know some surprising things about him.

God is full of surprises. Just when the house of David seemed to have withered and died, a new beginning was announced through the prophet Isaiah. From the stump of Jesse (David's father), a fresh green sprout, striking proof of life and vitality, was going to appear.

The promised sprout or bud would be a great leader, richly endowed with remarkable gifts of the Spirit. He would set up a wonderful kingdom, a kingdom like no other. And this is what Jesus did; he ushered in God's kingdom.

We marvel at Jesus' wisdom and understanding, and his passion for justice and right. He established a kingdom of peace so extraordinary that it could only be described in such striking images as lambs resting with wolves and cows with bears.

Jesus offered peace and unity in a troubled world. He offered this not only to Israel but to all the nations. Any promise from God is guaranteed to be fulfilled. What can we do to lay hold of such promises?

John the Baptizer, a prophet from the wilderness, confronted his hearers with the need for conversion, for a turning to God. He spoke harshly to those who thought it merely a matter of words. The Messiah to come would winnow the worthless chaff from genuine wheat. This was John's timeless warning, applicable in every age, especially in ours today.

Along with repenting and turning to God, Jesus promised that spiritual treasures can be found in the church through doing such things as praying and living out one's faith.

GOING HOME

Third Sunday of Advent

1. Isaiah 35:1-6, 10
2. James 5:7-10
3. Matthew 11:2-11

THE WORLD has often witnessed the uprooting of whole native populations. Nations defeated in wars could expect deportation and slavery. God's own people tasted defeat and exile, a bitter experience which left its mark on Israel's memory.

The Babylonian Exile lasted almost fifty years. Yet during those years, prophetic voices were heard announcing restoration and return. Those voices lifted the spirit of the people and awakened their hope by describing the return to their homeland in beautiful imagery. The return would be like strolling again through the forests of Lebanon or a joyful walk through the flowers of the valley of Sharon.

When we read these verses we see another deeper meaning in those words, for there are many kinds of return. The return from captivity also speaks eloquently of a spiritual return from the slavery of sin and estrangement from God.

Baggage is a concern for all travelers. In returning to God we need no earthly baggage, but rather hearts full of sorrow for our sins, and love for our kind, merciful, and patient God.

John the Baptizer thought Jesus should have gotten busy with the cleansing fire; he was puzzled with the Lord's timing. God's ways can be puzzling to us, but it is clear that he is interested in the growth of courage, confidence, and patience in his children.

Believers on their way "home" are joyful of heart and looking ahead. Their hearts are "steady" as St. James wrote.

The Advent wreath is a useful visual aid for this reality. The lighting of its candles, one by one, reminds us that God's light has slowly but steadily grown in the world, bringing us peace and reassurance as we draw closer to our heavenly home.

THE SIGN OF HIS LOVE
Fourth Sunday of Advent

1. Isaiah 7:10-14
2. Romans 1:1-7
3. Matthew 1:18-24

ONE IF THE MOST FAMOUS promises (or prophecies) ever made is found in Isaiah. The Lord was going to give to the house of Israel a *sign* as proof that he was actively interested in and committed to the well-being of his people.

The sign was, "… the virgin shall be with child and bear a son, … Immanuel," which means "God with us." It is worth noting that Isaiah spoke about "the" virgin. He was speaking of a specific one, someone quite special. King Ahaz' young wife did have a treasured son, Hezekiah, which means "the Lord is my strength," but the unusual solemnity of Isaiah's promise suggests that there is much more here than the proclamation of an ordinary birth. Christian tradition identifies "the virgin" as Jesus' mother, Mary.

It had to be a surprise, if not a shock, to St. Joseph when he noticed that his betrothed was with child. He did not think there was any wrongdoing on Mary's part, so Joseph could not find it in his heart to divorce her as an adulteress. She just did not fit the part. He decided it was better to simply respect the mystery and call off the wedding quietly.

Joseph's delicacy and fairness were to be richly rewarded. He learned that the child Mary was carrying had been conceived by the Holy Spirit. Isaiah's prophecy had come to a glorious, deeper fulfillment than just the birth of one king's son in ages past. God came as a Son to share in our human condition.

St. Paul presented Jesus to the Romans as God's Son, the one born of the line of David and proclaimed by the prophets. He, Paul, had been chosen to bring the Gentiles to faith in Jesus' name. Jesus came not only for the Israelites, but for all who would believe he was the Son of God. God invariably keeps his promises in astonishing ways. We are mystified and at the same time thrilled at the claims and assertions of our faith. Christmas reminds us every year how deeply God is committed to us, how richly he dwells in our midst, and how personally he loves us. We must be sure to return that love to him.

TWO

Christmas Season

A JOYFUL BIRTHDAY

Christmas (Midnight Mass),
December 25 [A,B,C]

1. Isaiah 9:1-6
2. Titus 2:11-14
3. Luke 2:1-14

ONE NIGHT, two thousand years ago, while silence covered the little town of Bethlehem, something wonderful happened. A child was born of a virgin named Mary.

For nine months, in the dark silence of her womb, the child had been forming, her Son and God's. Isaiah the prophet had spoken of this infant, noting that he would be endowed with special gifts of wisdom and power. Best of all, he would actually be the Prince of Peace.

At Bethlehem a great light shone out of the darkness. With the fullness of God's graciousness revealed, the world again knew laughter and gladness and joy. Christmas is God's gift to his children in every age, and it reminds us that we too are part of God's eternal plan. God's Son has taken our human nature upon himself.

Joy results when we receive a precious gift, the sign that someone loves us. God's gift of himself to us in the incarnation, in Jesus, is evidence of his bountiful love and goodness.

St. Luke tells us about Caesar Augustus and Quirinius, two impressive rulers of Rome and Syria. But it was because of this Jesus, born in Bethlehem to Mary, that the angels sang their *Gloria in excelsis* to God, Luke also records how Mary had wrapped her newborn Son in swaddling clothes and laid him in a manger. Shepherds came to see if the angels' proclamation was true. They saw a child lying in a manger and knew then that he was indeed Christ, the newborn King.

May our hearts be a manger where Christ the Lord will find a welcome. Then he will surely bring us lasting joy and peace.

A FAMILY CHOSEN BY GOD

Holy Family

1. Sirach 3:2-6, 12-14
2. Colossians 3:12-21
3. Matthew 2:13-15, 19-23

THE HOLY FAMILY consisted of Jesus, Mary, and Joseph. Although they were the chosen family of God, they were not spared from great trial and suffering. Joseph learned that Herod sought to kill Mary's child, so they fled to Egypt for safety. When Herod died, the family resettled again in Nazareth in Galilee. Joseph's death left Jesus fatherless and Mary widowed.

Neither Joseph nor Mary made the headlines in their lifetime. Their home, however, was notable for its many virtues. Its prevailing atmosphere was surely one of harmony and peace. There was also an ever-deepening awareness of God's plan and of their part in it. There was mystery and wonder, but no big fanfare.

There is much we can learn here and apply to our families. We often fail to communicate what we want to say, especially to those in our own family. Yet there are qualities in family life that we cherish deeply. One of these is loyalty; family members *belong* to one another individually, and are committed to the family as a whole. There is a deep and mysterious bond of love between them. They can do important things together like fellowship and prayer. The family that prays together, stays together.

Just so Sirach speaks of the solicitude and respect we should have towards our aging parents, following the theme of family life. Our placing them in convalescent homes may be a solution different from that of an earlier age. But times and cultures change. This decision can reflect a mature, responsible love for those who have borne and raised us. The key issue is to ask: Are we doing what is best and most loving in the circumstances for those we love?

As challenging as families can sometimes be, it is still a wonderful thing to grow up in one. Let us thank God for our own family, where we learned not only to receive but also to give of ourselves.

A MOTHER'S LOVE

Mary, Mother of God [A,B,C]

1. **Numbers 6:22-27**
2. **Galatians 4:4-7**
3. **Luke 2:16-21**

MOTHERHOOD is one of the great wonders of the world, the result of a profound mystery; the giving and sustaining of human life. Today, eight days after Christmas, we gather to celebrate the motherhood of the Virgin Mary. She is honored because, in the fullness of time, she brought God's very own Son into the world.

Mary's child was truly both God and man. This was something utterly unique. Because God became human in time through her, Mary is known as the *Theotokos* or God-bearer.

Jesus was "born of a woman, born under the law," wrote St. Paul. He became one suddenly limited by time and space. He was a baby receiving motherly love and care. It is impossible for us to measure the influence she had on him, but judging from his parables and the many references to the details of family life, it must have been considerable.

Although Mary's place in God's plan was special, she led a very human life. Her response, "May it be done to me according to your word," meant that she actually carried God as a baby in her womb for nine months. Her life was one of faith, a walk in the darkness of the mystery whose center was God. No wonder she "pondered over these things."

The word "blessed"—as in "Blessed be God"—expresses praise and admiration. Our "God bless you" is a petition that God will be pleased with and show his graciousness to a particular person. Blessed indeed was Mary, God's mother in Christ Jesus. We too have partaken in that graciousness. God has sent forth the Spirit of his Son into our hearts, and we can cry out to God as sons and daughters, "Abba! Father!" The first reading at today's Mass is a lovely prayer of blessing that is still used in Jewish synagogues.

We do well on this New Year's Day to recall the great things God has done for Mary, and through her what he has done for us.

GOD WITH US

Second Sunday after Christmas [A,B,C]

1. Sirach 24:1-4, 8-12
2. Ephesians 1:3-6, 15-18
3. John 1:1-18

A BEAUTIFUL piece of art captures our attention. To ponder it is a delight, and we marvel at the creative genius behind the work.

God is an artist too. According to his eternal plan, he came down to earth to reestablish a personal relationship between himself and his creation. We are forever grateful for such a demonstration of divine mercy for us.

The Lord Jesus came into the world, not as a grown man, but born of a woman just as we were. He entered the world as a tiny baby and grew into adulthood as we all did. His was not a hurried, overnight visit, but one that lasted for a lifetime!

Before Jesus' coming, inspired writers showed the various ways God was with his people on earth. God's presence, for example, was manifest to his people in Exodus as a cloud by day and a pillar of fire by night. Later, he took up residence in his people in Solomon's temple. God determined to maintain contact with Israel, his chosen people, throughout history. When God finally came to earth personally in human form, he was Jesus, filled with wisdom and endowed with divine power. In such wisdom personified, Christian scholars have recognized the prophetic foreshadowing and fulfillment of God's presence among his people throughout the ages.

According to this divine plan, we can become God's adopted children. And we are the temple in which he dwells continuously. What a revelation of God's love! Paul never tired of marveling at God's extravagance in sharing his very life with sinners.

Why should God bother to keep in touch with us? The only answer is because he is good and he is merciful. The first verses of the gospel of John tell us how the divine Word became flesh and inaugurated a close, personal relationship with us. Jesus, "Eternal Wisdom," opened the way for God to dwell with us and in us forever.

THE CHRISTMAS STAR

Epiphany [A,B,C]

1. Isaiah 60:1-6
2. Ephesians 3:2-3, 5-6
3. Matthew 2:1-12

TO GAZE AT STARS glowing brightly in the night sky is often a mesmerizing experience. We can imagine how shepherds in the night must relish the sight. Before such splendor many have been moved to think of God.

Today we celebrate the feast of Epiphany. The word means "appearance," or "manifestation," and refers to the glorious news that Christ, the newborn King, has come into the world.

Coming twelve days after Christmas, Epiphany is aptly called "Twelfth Night." With it we associate the Star of Bethlehem. It was a strange star that stopped and started, disappeared and then reappeared. Was it real? Were the Magi real people?

The Bible spoke of a star that would rise from Jacob, and many saw this as a prophecy of the star to come. Astrologers, as magi were sometimes called (not to be confused with astrologers today), might have seen it. Whether the Magi or the star were real or not, however, the focus of this story centers on Jesus and is rich in symbolism.

Jesus the Son of God had been born and come into the world to restore harmony between God and all his children. Not only shepherds and kings, but the very heavens proclaimed his glory and welcomed him. How better to do justice to this noble theme than to picture a supernatural star glowing in the heavens, guiding foreign kings to the feet of the newborn infant?

It is not easy to deal with divine matters. St. Paul had the privilege to be one of the first to proclaim this great mystery, hidden from all ages, to the world. The Star of David has appeared to us all, Jew and Gentile alike. This is the true message of Epiphany.

REMEMBERING OUR OWN BAPTISM

Baptism of the Lord

1. Isaiah 42:1-4, 6-7
2. Acts 10:34-38
3. Matthew 3:13-17

THE PROPHET Isaiah spoke four times of a mysterious servant who would bring justice to the nations, light to the world, and freedom from slavery. This servant's ministry would change the world.

The apostle Peter learned in a dream that God was not just for a specific people, but was to be Lord over all nations. He played no favorites, nor was he restricted geographically to any one place. He was Lord of the universe.

This extraordinary revelation was joyfully welcomed by Luke the evangelist, who was himself a Gentile. Peter's news was first made known in the house of the God-fearing Gentile, Cornelius.

Isaiah yearned for the day the heavens would be torn open and rain down the Just One. Emmanuel, "God with us," was to be Spirit-filled. In his kingdom peace would prevail, and the earth would be filled with knowledge of the Lord.

The Sinless One, Jesus, insisted that John the Baptist baptize him. It was a climactic moment in Jesus' life. He had grown in wisdom and grace into adulthood. Now about to enter his public ministry, he symbolically aligned himself with the sinful humanity he had come to redeem by choosing to be baptized.

In this decisive step, we see Jesus' insight into his earthly mission. He was knowingly assuming the responsibility he had been given by his heavenly Father. He had perceived that the Scriptures had spoken of his coming. Entering the waters of the Jordan, he was setting into motion the process that would inevitably lead to his death. Yet by his death alone, could we be redeemed.

At this baptism, a voice from heaven declared Jesus to be his "beloved Son." A dove, symbolic of God's Spirit, came down upon Jesus when he came up out of the water.

It is good to celebrate Jesus' baptism, for we are thus reminded of the magnificent gifts of grace Jesus has brought to us all. We should also remember our own baptisms as our first step on the road back to God.

THREE

Ordinary Time before Lent

THE SERVANT AND THE LAMB

Second Sunday of the Year

1. Isaiah 49:3, 5-6
2. 1 Corinthians 1:1-3
3. John 1:29-34

As WE BEGIN our journey through a new year, we are introduced to a mysterious servant of the Lord. Isaiah describes him as someone known to God long before he was born.

This servant was commissioned to restore a captive nation to its homeland. More than that, he was to be a light to the nations, fulfilling an astounding global mission. It shows us God has always had a plan for the future, for the times we live in now.

The age of biblical revelation has passed, but God is never without servants. St. Paul spoke of the church in Corinth and of the holy people of God there. Jesus was their Lord. Paul's letter could have been written to us who participate in God's plan today.

As Jesus approached the Jordan River, John the Baptist shouted these strange words, "Behold, the Lamb of God, who takes away the sins of the world." Why did he say such a thing? Why would he compare Jesus to a sheep?

A lamb was a very valuable animal in those days, not only commercially, but especially for religious purposes. A lamb was the sacrificial victim par excellence. By sacrificing a lamb, sins offensive to God were considered to be washed away and the covenant of divine friendship restored.

And there is something else. The strange mysterious Servant of the Lord was described by Isaiah as suffering death not for his own sins, but for the sins of others. It was an expiatory sacrifice.

What John was saying, then, is that Jesus had come as the Servant of God and, though sinless, would die on the cross for the sins of the world. A voice from heaven further enlightened John about Jesus. The descent of the Spirit on Jesus as John baptized him signaled the beginning of the messianic era. He was "the Chosen One of God."

We begin this year then with confidence renewed. Jesus, the Son of God and the Lamb of God will walk with us day by day if we continue to turn to him in trust and obedience.

THE MASTER'S CALL

Third Sunday of the Year

1. Isaiah 8:23—9:3
2. 1 Corinthians 1:10-13, 17
3. Matthew 4:12-23

THE KINGDOM established by David was torn apart after Solomon's death. The northern kingdom was ravaged by the Assyrians, and the Babylonians carried the southern nation into exile. The darkness for God's people would yield, though, so said a prophetic voice, to a great light in a time to come. Abundant joy and happiness would be restored. A king of peace would come to establish freedom forever.

St. Matthew portrayed Jesus as the King foretold by Isaiah. He was in fact a light shining in the darkened world. He preached repentance for the reign of God was at hand.

It is interesting that God, who needs nobody's help, entrusted his message and his plan to human beings. Walking one day beside the Sea of Galilee, Jesus singled out four men who were fisherman; Simon and Andrew, and two other brothers named James and John. All he said to them was "Come after me,..." and they did. They became his apostles, his ministers, and fishers of men.

What a tribute to Jesus' influence that his simple invitation was enough to make hardworking fishermen turn their backs on their livelihood and families to become his disciples.

There were challenges to the spread of the gospel from early on. Paul discovered that the Corinthians, for example, were given to boasting not so much about the gospel as about the preachers of the gospel—Paul, Apollos, Cephas, or Christ. Such fragmentation always produces bickering, quarrels, and division. Paul would not tolerate that. "Is Christ divided?," he wrote. It is Christ alone who matters. Only in him can true unity of faith be achieved and preserved.

Each of us is called by the Lord to live a holy life, to be like candles shining in the darkness of this world. We must be like fishermen, too, drawing others by our example to Christ and to his undivided church.

OUR BLUEPRINT FOR LIFE	**1. Zephaniah 2:3; 3:12-13**
Fourth Sunday of the Year	**2. 1 Corinthians 1:26-31**
	3. Matthew 5:1-12

FEW PEOPLE leave on a trip without getting advice. Whether it comes from parents or friends, it indicates that someone loves us and wishes us well.

The Bible is full of advice for travelers on their way back to God. The advice we receive is free, but we must humbly admit that we need it. Life and its problems are beyond the control of mere mortals like ourselves.

One never has to apologize for following good advice like, "Seek justice, seek humility;... take refuge in the name of the Lord: the remant of Israel...."

St. Paul noticed how in the battle between good and evil, God uses little people to shame the wise. God uses the simple to triumph over the strong. He uses those who are weak. It will thus be clear to all that the victory is due to God and not to human resources.

The Sermon on the Mount contains the beatitudes, that is, Jesus' recommendations on how to follow God on our journey through life. The beatitudes seem so simple, but they are almost shocking and not at all what we might expect. They upset our usual lines of thinking. Who are the lucky ones (the "blessed")? The poor in spirit are those whose confidence is in God who makes things turn out well for those who manifest compassion toward others, and those who are considerate are full of mercy and lovers of peace.

One never has to apologize for being good by following Jesus' blueprint for life. Virtue is not weakness. True strength is not just a matter of muscle. Those who are dear to God are deserving of admiration.

We thank God, then, for the good advice on gospel values that will bring us safely home and help make the world a better place.

LIGHTS IN THE DARKNESS

Fifth Sunday of the Year

1. Isaiah 58:7-10
2. 1 Corinthians 2:1-5
3. Matthew 5:13-16

WHAT A DIFFERENCE an individual can make! One person can enter a room and the whole place seems to brighten up. Another person in the group leaves and the atmosphere changes in tone again. We can each make a great impact on those around us. Together as a body of Christians, we can be even more powerful in effecting change.

Isaiah, an energetic leader, wrote for a people recently liberated from slavery in a foreign land. They returned to their beloved homeland free, yet things were difficult. Their land had been ravaged. The prophet had to remind them to share bread with the hungry and care for the needy, to truly be like lights shining in the darkness.

Religion is a social phenomenon, marked by a desire to serve God in union with others. People compete fiercely for material goods, but spiritual blessings can be shared peaceably by all and benefit everyone for the common good.

The apostles soon learned the power of the Word of God. Going into foreign lands, without any special training in teaching, philosophy, or debate, they simply told the good news. The power of the Spirit, however, was unleashed to convince and convict thousands.

Jesus said, "You are the salt of the earth." Salt has many specific qualities and useful purposes. We depend on salt daily. We use it for cooking, we put blocks of it out for wild animals, we spread it on roads for safer driving conditions, and so forth. The Romans taxed it in ancient times, and people were known to fight over it.

When put on food, of course, it is absorbed and its flavor spreads throughout. With salt, food has taste and savor, and is more easily preserved. Like salt, we can act as preservatives by being healthy influences in a perishing world. We can be spread out and make a wonderful difference for those who know us.

Jesus also called the apostles "the light of the world." By witnessing to Christ through their lives and preaching, these apostles dispelled the darkness of sin and generated divine life around them. Their goodness had a tremendous spiritual and social impact.

As Catholics we ought to be aware of the social dimensions of our faith. As good Catholics we can contribute much to the world.

CHOOSE LIFE

Sixth Sunday of the Year

1. Sirach 15:15-20
2. 1 Corinthians 2:6-10
3. Matthew 5:17-37

GOD NEVER gives anyone permission to sin, but he endows us with freedom that enables us either to obey his law and in so doing to choose life, or to break it and in so doing to choose death. We learn this from the Old Testament book of Sirach, but our own hearts also confirm it.

Such Christian wisdom is not a philosophy. It is a sober, reasoned view of life under a loving God who sent his Son into a sinful world to be its Savior.

Jesus' most famous sermon was given on a mountainside in Galilee. He addressed such highly explosive issues as the law (the Torah, plus the Talmud and Mishnah), murder, anger, adultery, and oaths.

For Jesus, love of God and neighbor was basic Christianity. He made it clear that these supreme laws were not being properly developed or understood. He even boldly set himself up as an authority greater than Moses. Was he then a revolutionary and an agitator? Not at all. "I have come not to abolish but to fulfill [the law]," he said. Jesus was not changing God's direction for his people, he was completing the Father's plan perfectly.

Jesus was no minimalist when it came to loving and worshiping God. His approach, in contrast to the dull, legalistic interpretations given by some of the Pharisees, sparkled with life. In order to fulfill the law, Jesus called for a new spiritual attitude toward God and neighbor. Without such a change, the law was losing its true value and meaning.

Jesus spoke about anger and adultery and divorce, always

emphasizing the importance of having the proper *inner* attitude. Sinful thoughts pave the way for sinful actions; these can and must be controlled. Jesus recommended taking an honest hard look at one's priorities. Nothing we hold dear can surpass in value our friendship with God and our love of neighbor. We must choose what is right and avoid doing wrong. Thankfully, we have God's grace and the power of the Holy Spirit to help us.

HOLINESS

Seventh Sunday of the Year

1. Leviticus 19:1-2, 17-18
2. 1 Corinthians 3:16-23
3. Matthew 5:38-48

NOT MANY PEOPLE are willing to talk about holiness. It seems an unpleasant topic since it is often associated with rigidity, self-denial, and not having fun. Holiness is often regarded as a "remote" concept, restricted to priests, women, and children. It's not for men, or for those interested in having an enjoyable life.

In point of fact, however, holiness is a really exciting topic, reminding us all that we are God's own children, made in his image and called out of one lifestyle to share in his life on this earth and forever in the next.

"The Lord said to Moses, 'Speak to the whole Israelite community and tell them: Be holy, for I the LORD your God, am holy.'"

Life in Christ involves love, mercy, and kindness toward others. Such attractive attributes are found in God and beautifully exemplified in Jesus Christ and the lives of his saints. For us, holiness means becoming more and more like Christ.

Holiness, then, is every Christian's calling. Jesus said "You must love the Lord your God... and your neighbor as yourself." To join these two separate commands into one was a stroke of genius. In so doing, Jesus revolutionized all religion.

Turning the other cheek and loving one's enemies clearly means that there is more to life than revenge and hatred. Jesus' words do not rule out justice, nor do they require an automatic enthusiasm for everybody. We are, however, not to wish harm on others, but to wish them well, and to be ready to help them if we can.

Jesus calls us to be good, to cultivate a noble mind, and pray for a compassionate heart. Wherever we Christians go, we bear Christ in us, sharing in his holiness and manifesting it to the world through the prayers, works, and sufferings of each day.

Holiness is our vocation, our business in life. It has a beauty all its own.

THE PROVIDENT GOD
Eighth Sunday of the Year

1. Isaiah 49:14-15
2. 1 Corinthians 4:1-5
3. Matthew 6:24-34

WHEN JESUS spoke, ears began to tingle. On a hillside in Galilee, he gave his famous Sermon on the Mount. The world still marvels at it. It was an astounding speech, introducing a radically different outlook on life and turning earthly values completely upside down. His words, however, jolted the world into hope.

Hope was a rare commodity in a country devastated by war and depleted by mass deportation. Zion felt the Lord had forgotten his people, but the prophet Isaiah knew better. Can a mother forget her baby? God never forgets. Trust in him.

St. Paul had learned not to rely too much on human judgment. As God's servant, he had energetically dispensed the divine mysteries knowing he could not please everyone. He put little stock in his personal success, trusting God to judge him and his work. He is an excellent example for us.

Jesus taught that we should put our confidence in God rather than in material possessions. Jesus said not to worry too much about the future, for the Lord, who takes care of the birds of the air and the lilies of the field, will surely not neglect his children. Our heavenly Father knows what we need.

Jesus' message is very relevant in our own materialistic culture where too much emphasis is placed on acquiring possessions and status, so we can look good in the eyes of others. Also the more we have the more anxious we can become about losing it in the future. Thus, our success in the world's eyes quickly becomes an anxious burden, instead of bringing true freedom and happiness.

Divine providence can always be counted on. We must trust in God who always has us in his care and on his heart. We work and hope, not forgetting God.

BLESSED BY GOD

Ninth Sunday of the Year

1. Deuteronomy 11:18, 26-28
2. Romans 3:21-25, 28
3. Matthew 7:21-27

WHAT IS GOD saying to us this Sunday? Through the words of Moses, God reminds us to take his words seriously, for the decisions we make today indicate whether we are choosing life or death, a blessing or a curse.

A blessing is a sign of God's approval and favor. Life itself is a great blessing; eternal life, the great reward. A thing is cursed when it arouses God's anger and calls for punishment.

Jesus tells us that faith is not something we keep in a box, but in our hearts. Believers should be genuine and committed doers, not just talkers.

We do not become God's friends by merely observing laws, genuflecting, or making the sign of the cross. Faith is a gift of God, an initial gift we cannot earn. We can choose to receive the gift, however, and in so doing we become believers. To be *justified* means that we become blessed or pleasing in God's sight.

Once introduced into the state of grace, we can grow in it. We do this by working at being good—performing good works out of love for God and neighbor. Our spiritual life is dynamic, ever changing, and growing.

Jesus gave some sound advice about how to build a house for God. He, of course, is speaking about how to build and lead a strong spiritual life. It has to have a solid foundation. Jesus himself is that foundation. His words are words of eternal life.

The person who does the will of the Father in heaven and acts on those words will find favor in God's sight. Words alone, like a breath of wind, have no value without actions that follow them.

Moses, Paul, and Jesus tell us the facts of our spiritual life. Without God we are nothing, but with him we can do great things.

FOUR

Lenten Season

HEARTFELT REPENTANCE
Ash Wednesday [A,B,C]

1. Joel 2:12-18
2. 2 Corinthians 5:20-6:2
3. Matthew 6:1-6, 16-18

EXTERNAL WORKS of repentance have no value in themselves. God calls us to repent and experience a deep conversion of the heart. If we place too much emphasis on external works, to the detriment of our spiritual life, we easily begin to slide into hypocrisy. Lent is like a trumpet blast calling us back to the basics of the spiritual life: penance, alms, fasting, and—above all—prayer of the heart.

In the oriental symbolism of regret, Joel tells the sinful people of Israel "to rend [their] hearts, not [their] garments." Joel is describing here the symbolic rending of one's garments in Jewish tradition as a posture of grief and repentance over one's sins. Joel sounds a note of urgency in using this turn of phrase to call for heartfelt repentance. He commands the blowing of a trumpet and the proclamation of an assembly and a fast for the whole people.

This is exactly what occurs each Lenten Season. The entire church is called to spend forty days, focused not so much on works of penance, as upon a wholehearted return to God alone.

A similar note of urgency marks the apostle Paul's second letter to the Corinthians. In emphatic speech, he reminds his listeners not to put off being reconciled to God. He underscores that since the Lord Jesus has come and delivered us from sin, now—not at some point in the future—is the day of salvation! Now is the time to turn back to God!

Jesus describes the hypocrisy that results if we do not respond to God's grace and turn back to him. We become hypocrites who perform religious acts for others to see. We must guard against such an empty, outward show by not announcing to others the good we do. Instead, we should wait for God's eternal reward, which will be beyond our imagining.

TEMPTATIONS

First Sunday of Lent

1. Genesis 2:7-9; 3:1-7
2. Romans 5:12-19
3. Matthew 4:1-11

WHEN ADAM AND EVE disobeyed God, they did not at once fall down dead. They did, however, lose the priceless treasure of friendship with God. Sin has a high price tag on it.

Jesus, the Second Adam, undid Adam's sin by dying on the cross. St. Paul noted that the grace gained therein far surpassed the original fall and its consequences.

Jesus was "tempted by the devil." Matthew and Luke vouch for this. The temptations took place inwardly where, like all people, Jesus had a mind, an imagination, and a genuinely free will.

The things presented to Jesus as temptations were not evil in themselves, but good food, reliance on the loving care of God, authority and prestige. What was wrong, then, in being offered these things? It was wrong to suggest to Jesus that he should and could fulfill his human needs apart from God. It was wrong to have him call upon God simply to "test" God's goodness and power. It would be wrong for Jesus to live for the sake of money and position.

There is a lesson in this for us. By God's grace and our choosing, we can resist the powers of evil. Free will is a truly astounding gift. Notice how in the Gospel account each of the temptations ends with the devil urging Jesus, "Do it!" Jesus resisted him. We too can choose to resist the devil and his temptations.

The challenge for us is to make the right choices. Many of us fall into temptation out of boredom or restlessness. Drugs seem to promise a world of excitement. Or sometimes we're looking for a quick answer. We may think alcohol can dull the pain and ugliness of life. What lies these are!

Jesus was tempted to show us that we too can use the strength God has given us to live a life pure and pleasing to him. We must keep our eyes always turned toward heaven where our eternal home is. Lent is a time to reflect upon this lesson.

THE PRELUDE TO GLORY

Second Sunday of Lent

1. Genesis 12:1-4
2. 2 Timothy 1:8-10
3. Matthew 17:1-9

GOD MADE a promise to Abraham. He told Abraham that if he left his homeland for a strange and alien country a great destiny awaited him. Trusting in God, Abraham obeyed.

It took courage for Abraham to set forth on such a journey, one fraught with unknown perils and hardships. Yet his mission resulted in repercussions felt throughout the whole world and throughout the ages. As God promised, Abraham's descendants would, in time, carry the news about God to the ends of the earth.

Some of the simplest undertakings entail various sorts of hardships. The same is true of spiritual undertakings. St. Paul advised Timothy to be ready for his share of difficulties while doing God's work. God would see his plan through, however, for the sake of the gospel and out of his love for Timothy personally.

Jesus spoke about his coming death on three different occasions. On one such occasion, on top of Mount Tabor, he unveiled to his chosen three disciples, Peter, James, and John, the glory of his soul shining through his human body. To see the face of God as he did was enough to transfigure even his garments!

Peter was thrilled to see his master speaking with Moses and Elijah and to hear the voice from heaven saying, "This is my beloved Son, with whom I am well pleased; listen to him." Eager to prolong this marvelous moment, this glimpse of glory, he offered to set up tents for these three holy prophets.

The vision quickly faded, however, and the apostles found themselves alone with Jesus once again. Jesus then instructed them not to tell others about the vision until the Son of Man rose from the dead.

In all this there is much food for thought. We should realize that although there can be moments of hardship, suffering, and even ultimately death in this life, God has promised a glory to come. An unending transfiguration awaits those who walk with Jesus.

THE WATER OF NEW LIFE

Third Sunday of Lent

1. Exodus 17:3-7
2. Romans 5:1-2, 5-8
3. John 4:5-42

SYMBOLIC language permeates the Bible. Concrete signs carry important spiritual meaning. Important truths can be effectively communicated through symbols, as we learn from Jesus' own teaching in parables.

We know something about hunger and thirst. We eat and drink to stay alive. Food and water symbolize life. But what kind of life are we preserving? Jesus comes to offer us food and drink that leads to eternal life.

When the Israelites complained they were dying of thirst, Moses, at God's bidding, struck the rock, and abundant water gushed forth. Do we see a connection between water and the Lord, who is spirit and life?

St. Paul saw it. Water enables the earth to bring forth fruit. So too it is with the grace of God. It is *poured* into our hearts by the Holy Spirit, enabling us to bring forth fruits of faith, hope, and love.

Water attains its own level based on its flow from a particular source. The grace of God is like water in that sense. It comes from on high, but seeks to return to its source, which is God. "… while we were still sinners," Paul says, Christ showed his love for us by dying for us, bringing us back to God from whom we were alienated by our sins. Washed clean of sin and guilt, we are borne heavenward, to life with God.

When Jesus asked a Samaritan woman for a drink of water, a remarkable dialogue began. Jesus assured the woman that he could give a water that banished thirst forever. Intrigued, she asked for some of it, and learned that he, Jesus, was the Living Water that springs up to eternal life.

Water—life; grace—everlasting life. Lent is a time for grace, for dialogue with God, for growing closer to God in spirit and in truth. The life-giving waters of baptism and all the sacraments keep us close to Christ, the source of life.

LIGHT FOR SEEING

Fourth Sunday of Lent

1. 1 Samuel 16:1, 6-7, 10-13
2. Ephesians 5:8-14
3. John 9:1-41

"LIGHT" is one of the most common words used to describe physical or spiritual illumination. "Light" reveals both the material world around us as well as spiritual truths within us.

Darkness too has many forms. A searching Samuel was groping in the dark, looking for a king to replace Saul. The light increased, and he found and anointed David, son of Jesse, as king.

Darkness also signifies a life of sin. It is a moral blindness, unable to distinguish between right and wrong, good and bad. Paul reminds the Ephesians that they had once been in darkness, but now were "light in the Lord." They had welcomed the gospel and received baptism. Their lives should now reflect that grace.

In healing the man born blind, Jesus made use of some very earthy substances. He spat on the ground and made a muddy paste. That must have been little short of shocking for many. Questions must have been raised in the minds and hearts of many of his onlookers. Seeing, for many in this case, was not believing. On the other hand, hearing Jesus' claim to be the Son of Man, the blind man cried out, "I do believe, Lord." He had received spiritual insight.

Lent calls on us to reexamine our way of life in the light of the gospel. We must listen to the voice of our conscience and take steps to improve our lifestyle.

God does not ask us to do extraordinary things so much as to make use of the means he has already provided for us: prayer, confession, and Holy Communion. Through these, we open our eyes and our lives to the divine Light which we share with our brothers and sisters in Christ.

DRY BONES AND LIFE

Fifth Sunday of Lent

1. Ezekiel 37:12-14
2. Romans 8:8-11
3. John 11:1-45

THE PROPHET Ezekiel had a vision where he saw a valley filled with dry bones, clattering in the wind. A voice asked: "Can these bones come to life?" He answered cautiously, "Lord God, you alone know that." Then as the prophet watched in awe, life was breathed into the bones and they came together, forming a vast army.

This vision fanned the flame of hope among the exiles. God would breathe into them a new spirit and restore them to life as a people in their own land once again. It was like being given a new lease on life.

The vision speaks to us too. Our world is full of shattered hopes, disillusionment, and disappointment. Friends fail us, plans go awry, or our dreams never materialize. Our lives seem filled with dry bones. But there is hope.

St. Paul advises against living "in the flesh" as if there was nothing else to live for. For us, there is a life "in the spirit" as well. The Spirit of God, breathed into us at baptism, enables us to see and to appreciate a new life and a new way of living.

Jesus is himself the source of life. With tears in his eyes, he stood before the tomb of his friend, Lazarus. He commanded the stone to be removed from the tomb and cried out, "Lazarus, come out!" The dead man was resurrected and came forth. Life had been breathed back into dry bones.

Jesus is clearly the Master of life and death. Raising Lazarus from the dead was an astounding sign of divine power. With Jesus, death is not the end, but only a step leading to a new, wonderful life. We cannot even imagine what things God has prepared for those who love him.

Throughout Lent we hear the Lord urging us to "come out" from the dark tomb of our sins, to be free, and to live with him.

WHAT PART DO WE PLAY?

Passion (Palm) Sunday

1. Isaiah 50:4-7
2. Philippians 2:6-11
3. Matthew 26:14—27:66

JESUS' LIFE, death, and resurrection touched many lives, not excluding our own. Let us see how and where we fit into the story.

Judas Iscariot betrayed his master. Why? Was it out of loyalty to Moses and the law? To force Jesus' hand and make him seize the reins of power? To save his own skin by siding with the enemy and to make a little money while he was at it?

Until he died, Peter would remember the three times he denied knowing Christ. He would also remember the Master's mercy and forgiveness.

Pontius Pilate was governor of Judea for ten years (A.D. 26-36). He was to collect the emperor's taxes and to keep order. A rough and ready man, he found himself enmeshed in a complicated situation for which he was ill-prepared. In the end he washed his hands of innocent blood and gave in to the demands of the Jewish leaders and the people.

Barabbas, a known murderer and thief, became a hero to an unruly crowd, was preferred over Jesus, and found himself set free. His unexpected choice was engineered in part by a handful of scribes and Pharisees.

Such was the cast of characters who had parts to play in a drama of cosmic proportions. Which characters do we identify with *and why?* Jesus still occupies center stage. Some two thousand years ago he entered Jerusalem in triumph, "hosanna's" ringing in his ears, palm branches waving all about.

He deserved it all. He was the Servant of the Lord, taking upon himself the sins of the world. His death wiped away the enormous debt humanity had incurred by sin. His obedience to his Father was so perfect that it more than sufficed to restore us to God's friendship.

During these days we once again renounce our sinful behavior and resolve to align ourselves, not with sinners, but with Christ who died for us. He rose from the dead, invested now with a divine title: Lord. He deserves our grateful thanks.

THE LAST SUPPER
Holy Thursday [A,B,C]

1. Exodus 12:1-8, 11-14
2. 1 Corinthians 11:23-26
3. John 13:1-15

IF YOU KNEW you were to die in less than twenty-four hours, how would you spend your last hours? Jesus knew his hours were numbered, so we have cause to pay special attention to the things he said the night before he died, at that Last Supper.

At the Last Supper Jesus instituted the Eucharist, made his apostles priests, washed their feet, and in solemn words sought to console and hearten them.

The Last Supper recalled the covenant God had made with his people long ago. In God's plan, the old covenant was intended as a sign of an even greater covenant God was to make and seal with the blood of his own Son, Jesus.

We have heard again, in the earliest account of the institution of the Eucharist, how Jesus said over the bread, "This is my body," and over the wine, "This cup is the new covenant in my blood." He then instructed the apostles to do what he had done (the present imperative can be translated "Keep on doing this") and to always do so "in remembrance of me."

God thus devised a marvelous way to be always with his children. Jesus was not just a beautiful memory, but was to dwell with the faithful as life-giving food and drink. As a further legacy, he set for us an unforgettable example: he washed the feet of his new priests. How could they ever forget that they were to serve others in humility after such an experience?

The Eucharist is our way to an intimate, personal union with our Savior. With each celebration of the Eucharist we can be nourished with his body and blood. Incredible? Yes, but so it is. We treasure our Masses and our priests, for as St. Peter said, "Lord, you have the words of eternal life."

BEHOLD YOUR SAVIOR

Good Friday [A,B,C]

1. Isaiah 52:13—53:12
2. Hebrews 4:14-16; 5:7-9
3. John 18:1—19:42

BEHOLD YOUR SAVIOR, the suffering Servant of Yahweh, who was "pierced for [your] offenses, crushed for [your] sins." He is the great High Priest who offered "prayers and supplications with loud cries and tears to God" on your behalf. He is the Master who was denied, betrayed, and deserted by his followers. He is the true King of the Jews who suffered false judgment and the penalty of death at the hands of his own people and the Roman authorities.

Yet God has performed an awesome, marvelous work in allowing his own Son to undergo such suffering and mistreatment. For behold, the Crucified One shall "take away the sins of many, and win pardon for [our] offenses." Behold, because of this great High Priest having gone before us and having suffered and been tested in every way like us, we can "confidently approach the throne of grace." Behold, from the Savior's pierced side, flows forth blood and water, symbolic of the birth of the church from the side of the new Adam.

It is right and fit that we should meditate on the great triumph of the cross on Good Friday. It should both sober us and fill us with a reverential joy that God has graced us with so great a Redeemer. In light of God's great gift, what is our response? What can possibly be our response except to give ourselves without reserve to him who has given his all for us!

United to Mary, then, who has been given to us as our mother, let each of us say our yes to God. Let each of us hold nothing back as we confidently approach the throne of grace. Let us stand at the foot of the cross with Mary and reflect on this awesome event that confounded—and confounds for all time—the forces of darkness.

FIVE

Easter Season

TRIUMPH OVER DEATH
Easter Sunday [A,B,C]

1. Acts 10:34, 37-43
2. Colossians 3:1-4
3. John 20:1-9

EASTER, prepared for by six weeks of prayer, fasting, and penance, is the most important Christian feast of the year. It is ushered in with great pomp and circumstance.

The Easter Vigil is always impressive. First the fire is blessed at the back of the church, then the flaming Paschal candle is brought into the church and shared. Candles flicker to life in the darkness, the proclamation of Easter is sung in the *Exultet,* and a rich Old Testament tapestry is unfolded before the faithful. Water is blessed, and baptismal vows are renewed by all.

Next, with a blare of trumpets and triumphant song, the Mass begins. Alleluias fill the air. The Lord is praised for his victory over sin and death. Is it not marvelous that we have so great a Redeemer and are united with him?

The apostles had seen Christ die. Then three days later he appeared in their midst, miraculously raised from the dead. He ate with them, instructed them, and finally even conferred on them their global mission. After such manifest power from on high, nothing but death could stop them from preaching the resurrection.

The resurrection was the central theme of St. Paul's preaching. As he wrote to the Colossians, we have been brought back to true life with Christ by our baptism, and now share with him in every spiritual blessing from heaven. Praise the Lord.

Mary Magdalene was like an apostle to the apostles, bringing them news about the open, empty tomb. Peter and John ran to the tomb to see for themselves. It was just as she said. In the tomb there was no body, only the winding-cloths and face-cloth that were neatly folded and put to one side. Then they too believed that Jesus had been raised from the dead.

Lazarus and the widow of Nain's son were brought back to life too, but they eventually died again. Jesus, however, was the first-born from the dead. He was raised up to life, never to die again. Now he sits in glory at the right hand of God. Living with him now, we also hope to praise him face to face one day in heaven.

CHRISTIAN COMMUNITY	1. Acts 2:42-47
Second Sunday of Easter	2. 1 Peter 1:3-9
	3. John 20:19-31

WHILE THE REST of the world seemed to go on as usual after Jesus rose from the dead, something extraordinary was actually taking place that would change the course of history forever. The apostles were daily going to the temple to pray and to preach, but a new spirit animated them and all who listened. They were being bound together with new power and zeal and commitment. They were becoming the first Christian community.

This community did more than attend religious services together; their hearts were opened to share all their earthly goods with any others who joined them. Together they boldly prayed in public. Their houses were true places of fellowship for the break-ing of the bread. The Lord blessed them, and day by day their numbers swelled.

What they held in common was the conviction that they had each been born again, having died and been raised in baptism in union with Christ himself. Only this sure hope and the promise of life everlasting sustained them in the trials that were soon to test them as they worked out their salvation.

Jesus had appeared to his disciples late on Easter day. He wished them peace and then commissioned them into the world. He breathed on them and said, "Receive the Holy Spirit. If you forgive men's sins, they are forgiven them;..." The apostles must have listened in amazement.

How can mortal men forgive sins? They can only do so as

instruments of God, and only because God has revealed his intention that they do so. He made this clear in so many words. The Sacrament of Penance is the response of the community to Jesus' words. Did he mean to institute such a sacrament? Of course. As St. Augustine wrote, "If he did not mean to give his disciples this power, why did he say that he did?"

Thomas the apostle was gently chided for his lack of belief in Jesus' resurrection. "Blest are they who have not seen and have believed," responded Jesus to his proclamation of faith. Faith does not require "seeing," but acceptance of God's revelation.

It is comforting to know that we "belong" to a wonderful church. Here we share our faith with others who likewise seek to know, love, and praise God. How wonderful to get involved in God's own enterprise, to be able to confess our sins, and to be forgiven.

THE STORY OF EMMAUS

Third Sunday of Easter

1. Acts 2:14, 22-28
2. 1 Peter 1:17-21
3. Luke 24:13-35

THE FIRST of St. Peter's five sermons in Luke's *Acts of the Apostles* was given on the first Pentecost.

Peter, a forceful speaker, confidently explained that Jesus' death was part of God's plan; without it, the power of God and the sinlessness of Jesus could not have been demonstrated by his resurrection from the dead. The promise hinted at by David in Psalm 16 was thus magnificently fulfilled. Peter went on to say that it was this same Jesus who had sent the Holy Spirit to be with the church for all ages.

Peter also wrote two letters to the church. In the first letter he emphasized the cosmic and eternal significance of Jesus' death. By the blood of Jesus, the spotless Lamb, the breach between God and humanity has been mended. We now live in a new era of grace.

Peter explained that the pagan way of life, aimed at pleasure and the acquisition of this world's goods, was empty indeed, especially when compared to the wonderful alternative now available—a life of faith, hope, and love, the Christian way of life.

St. Luke tells the moving story of two disciples who shortly after Jesus' death, were walking toward a little town called Emmaus. On the way Jesus joined them! They did not recognize him. On hearing of their disappointment over the death of Jesus, the Lord opened their understanding to the many passages in the Scriptures that had predicted it. As he spoke, time slipped away. The travellers asked Jesus to eat with them and he agreed. They were richly rewarded. He revealed himself to them by opening their eyes at table in the breaking of the bread.

Just as with these two disciples, Jesus makes himself known to us in the proclaiming of the Word and the breaking of the bread each Sunday.

SHEPHERD OF OUR SOULS

Fourth Sunday of Easter

1. Acts 2:14, 36-41
2. 1 Peter 2:20-25
3. John 10:1-10

AFTER THE FIRST Pentecost, Peter was no longer a cowardly lion who denied Christ three times out of fear for his own life. He proclaimed Jesus' message in public with boldness and authority. The message was, however, the surprising invitation to repent and be baptized. Such had been Jesus' first public utterance. It is Christianity's challenging but joyful theme song.

The Holy Spirit, sent by Jesus as he promised, gave the apostles a profound new understanding of life. Jesus had not only suffered and died for our sins, but had shown us how to endure the sufferings, often undeserved, of this life.

Why must we suffer? Suffering is unavoidable in this life, for we are not living in paradise. If, however, we bear our sufferings patiently, they will lead us back to the Shepherd and Guardian of our souls.

Jesus once described himself as the gate of the sheepfold. It is a comforting picture. The shepherd of old kept night watch over his flocks. No one could approach his sheep to harm them. Then each morning he would lead his flock to water and pasture. In his presence they were safe day and night.

Always being in the care and company of Jesus is both a delightful and comforting truth. One cannot help but think of the church today, the sheepfold watched over by Christ and through whom believers enter into his company. Did he not say, "I came that they might have life and have it to the full"?

The Good Shepherd is always available. The sheep may often stray from him; then they must remember to do penance and turn from their sins. Only then will they know true peace and contentment.

SERVANTS OF THE LORD

Fifth Sunday of Easter

1. Acts 6:1-7
2. 1 Peter 2:4-9
3. John 14:1-12

AFTER the resurrection of Jesus, the church grew by leaps and bounds. With that increase, however, came practical problems. As a response to these growing church needs, after first seeking divine guidance, the apostles laid hands upon seven deacons to bless them as they were given the responsibility to handle practical concerns. A hierarchy of authority and function was thus organized and put in place early in church life.

All the faithful working together form a marvelous structure which rests upon Christ. Jesus is the Living Stone, rejected by humanity, but chosen by God, upon which all work must be built for God's kingdom and glory.

St. Peter declared all believers also to be God's "royal priesthood." It suggests that each member of the church has a vocation to lead a fruitful and holy life, one marked by a willingness to serve both God and neighbor. The church is the chosen race for God, a new Israel set apart and consecrated to God for the praise of his glory.

At the Last Supper, Jesus said, "Do not let your hearts be troubled." Although he was leaving them, he promised that there would be room for his friends wherever he was. His being with God would not rule out their seeing and being with him.

One apostle, Thomas, was not convinced, so Jesus said, "I am the way, and the truth, and the life;..." Strange, profound words to be pondered reverently. Jesus the Gate now calls himself the Way. This is metaphorical language. He is the entrance to life and the direction to follow. Where does Jesus lead us? He leads us into the truth of God. The Divine Word knows the Father and reveals him to us.

Jesus is also the Light, opening eyes to the splendor of God's plan of salvation and to the beauty and richness of the Lord. We who are the living stones of his church, praise and thank the Lord for letting us serve him.

THE ENDURING GOSPEL

Sixth Sunday of Easter

1. Acts 8:5-8, 14-17
2. 1 Peter 3:15-18
3. John 14:15-21

THE TECHNOLOGICAL AGE we live in allows news to travel fast. What happens on the other side of the world is known to us almost as soon as it occurs. Two thousand years ago, however, mass communication and modern transit did not exist to assist the passing on of any news of import. Yet Christianity was preserved and so spread throughout the world that even we in the twentieth century can now hear and receive the same wonderful message as those first believers did in Jerusalem so long ago.

The message that God sent his Son, the Lord Jesus, into our world to save us is still good news. The reality of having a risen Savior sparked the tremendous missionary outreach that has spanned seas and mountains and centuries of time.

Philip, for example, was one of the first missionaries who preached the gospel message in Samaria. News of this brought Peter and John from Jerusalem. When they saw the many Samaritans who believed, Peter and John baptized them, prayed with them, and saw them filled with the Holy Spirit. And so it was for thousands as missionaries went forth to preach the gospel with power.

The gospel has endured despite great opposition. A calm, reasonable statement of what Christians believe, coupled with lives based upon that faith, makes a strong case for Christianity. But it is really God's faithfulness to humanity that has preserved the gospel for so long. Every age needs and has produced, by the mercy of God, wonder-filled men and women of faith.

Jesus spoke five times about the Paraclete. The word means an advocate, or helper, or mediator. He was himself our Advocate, but promised to send another to take his place. These were both reassuring and revelational words. For one of Christianity's greatest mysteries, the Trinity, was thus being introduced for the first time. The Paraclete is, of course, the Third Person of the Godhead. These precious words about the indwelling of the Trinity in those who love and obey God's commandments were heard at the Last Supper as well.

God is indeed, through his Holy Spirit, with us through all the ages. The great news of the wonders God has given us and has prepared for us fills every good Christian with joy and wonder.

JESUS ENTERS INTO GOD'S PRESENCE

Ascension Thursday

1. Acts 1:1-11
2. Ephesians 1:17-23
3. Matthew 28:16-20

THE GREAT Doctor of the Church, St. Augustine, considered today's feast the greatest of them all, for it marked Jesus' entrance into a new and glorious condition of being.

In Matthew's version of the ascension account, Christ appears to the eleven apostles on a mountain before he is taken up into heaven. This mountaintop experience recalls for Matthew's Jewish readers other great manifestations of God—such as God's appearance to Moses on Mount Sinai, the delivery of Jesus' great sermon on a mountain (Matthew 5), and the transfiguration of Jesus on a mountain as well (Matthew 17).

Moreover, in Jesus' final address to the apostles, he commissions them to make disciples of all peoples, to baptize believers, and to teach those same believers everything the Lord has commanded the apostles. This great commission of the apostles is Christ's final work on earth before he is taken up into glory.

In Acts, Luke tells us that Jesus was lifted up before their eyes. The "up" is not primarily spatial; it essentially means that Jesus entered into God's presence in heaven. A cloud received him out of the apostle's sight.

The ascension does not imply that Jesus suddenly became inactive or disinterested in earthly affairs. Quite the contrary. Jesus sent the Holy Spirit from heaven to be with us as God's continual presence. Even now, Jesus is ever active, making constant intercession for us at the right hand of the Father.

Jesus did take a glorified human body with him into heaven. His body was both an instrument of our redemption, and a testimony to our worth. In heaven Jesus wears it still. When Jesus comes again, he will appear in that same glorified humanity.

The ascension filled the apostles with great joy, for they were now convinced that the Master was divine. Soon to be baptized in the Spirit, they would then begin their mission of carrying the good news to the whole world and to initiate all nations into the mystery of faith through baptism in water.

The ascension had also, as Paul perceived, a cosmic dimension, for it spelled the overthrow of demonic powers. It was further proof that Jesus was ruler of all things and head over all.

St. Augustine was right. The feast of the ascension is a truly glorious feast, the crowning touch to the death and resurrection of Jesus the Lord.

THE PRAYERFUL CHRISTIAN

Seventh Sunday of Easter

1. Acts 1:12-14
2. 1 Peter 4:13-16
3. John 17:1-11

THE END of one thing is always the beginning of another. We are now at the end of the joyful Easter season and must once again face the ordinariness of life. How we approach our lives now is as important as how we celebrated Easter.

After the ascension, the apostles stayed close together in the Upper Room with Mary and the other women. They awaited the Spirit whom Jesus promised to send. All were of one mind, as St. Luke notes, as they prayed together. It was the first retreat ever held.

After Pentecost, life went on as usual, but something new had been added. Pagans considered human suffering a calamity, subject to the whims of the gods. But Christians could now look upon suffering as a privilege, as an opportunity to imitate Christ. Suffering could now be accepted patiently, with an eye on the glory that is to come.

Daily sins and transgressions deserve punishment, but to suffer for doing *good* was not something to be ashamed of. Prayerful Christians, faced with many kinds of trials, can grow in virtue as they are purified by the fire.

Jesus, the perfect example, approached his passion with extraordinary composure. In his inspiring prayer to his heavenly Father, Jesus spoke to God of his work on earth. He was returning to the glory he shared with his Father since the beginning, but behind him he was leaving a marvelous new community, a church, through which eternal life could be gained by those who believed in him.

Jesus also prayed earnestly for his disciples. They had been the Father's gift to him. He was leaving them now, but they were to remain in the world to carry on his work.

We too were in Jesus' mind as he prayed, for with the help of the Holy Spirit, we carry on the work of the apostolic church.

THE CHURCH'S BIRTHDAY

Pentecost Sunday [A,B,C]

1. Acts 2:1-11
2. 1 Corinthians 12:3-7, 12-13
3. John 20:19-23

WE CELEBRATE the birthday of the church on the Jewish holiday of Pentecost. Fifty days after Jesus had risen from the dead, the disciples had gathered together to pray in the Upper Room. Suddenly, they heard the sound of a great wind and saw mysterious tongues of fire coming to rest on their heads. Wind and fire are biblical symbols indicating the presence of God. God's presence had indeed come to the disciples in a new and special way.

On Pentecost, God's birthday present to his church was the incredible, divine gift of the Holy Spirit. In the strength and power of the Spirit, the apostles became eloquent, courageous, dedicated mouthpieces and instruments of God.

Many centuries have since elapsed, but the church is still endowed with the charismatic gifts that marked her beginning. The most startling of these are perhaps the gifts of tongues and of healing.

Some divine gifts are designed and given for the good of the recipient, and these we call sanctifying graces. Charismatic gifts, on the other hand, are given for the good of the whole community, to draw attention to God and to his church.

God frequently comes to us bearing gifts. When Jesus appeared to the apostles in the Upper Room, wearing his wounds, he imparted to them immense inner peace and joy. He then made the startling statement, "Receive the Holy Spirit. If you forgive men's sins, they are forgiven them;..."

The Sacrament of Reconciliation is thus of divine, not human origin. As St. Augustine asked, "If Jesus did not mean to confer the power to forgive sins, why did he say that he did?" This is just one more precious gift of the Holy Spirit for the blessing of God's people.

Ordinary Time after Easter

THE MYSTERY OF THE TRINITY

Trinity Sunday

1. Exodus 34:4-6, 8-9
2. 2 Corinthians 13:11-13
3. John 3:16-18

THE THREE MAIN religions in the West and Middle East share a belief in one God. The Jews call him "Yahweh," the Muslims "Allah," and Christians, "God." There is, however, as we know, a significant difference in the beliefs about what kind of God he is.

Christianity differs from the other religions believing that God is Three-in-One. He has revealed himself to be Father, Son, and Holy Spirit. Each of the three divine persons is separate and distinct, yet each totally possesses the one divine nature. A Catholic often makes the Sign of the Cross, a specifically Christian profession of belief in the Triune God.

Articles of Faith are carefully worded expressions of belief in and respect for revealed truth. From the Trinity we learn that God is personal—an intelligent being who is loving, tender, compassionate, patient, and merciful. He is a moral God, moved by good rather than evil. He is intolerant of sin yet slow to anger. He is consistent and rational, not arbitrary or capricious. He is the omnipotent, immortal One; he is the invisible Creator of the universe.

The church has always believed in the Trinity. St. Paul, at the end of today's epistle, coined the phrase with which we often begin Mass (2 Corinthians 13:14). It reminds us of God the Father's great generosity, for he has given us his Son and the Holy Spirit as well as his very self.

Jesus once preached a sermon to Nicodemus, the Jewish ruler who visited him secretly at night. God so loved the world, Jesus told him, that he gave his only Son to bring eternal life to those who believe in him.

In comprehending divine mysteries, we seek to avoid extremes. The Trinity can never be wholly understood, but neither is it simply unintelligible nonsense. God has revealed enough about the Trinity for us to grasp the awesomeness, lavishness, and creativity of a loving God. If we cannot wholly comprehend, we can at least be wholly grateful for an ever present God. In the next life, we shall see God and understand more fully. But for now we are free to marvel at the immensity and harmony of God who is Three-in-One.

THE GREAT SACRAMENT

The Body and Blood of Christ

1. Deuteronomy 8:2-3, 14-16
2. 1 Corinthians 10:16-17
3. John 6:51-58

ALTAR BOYS in tunics and surplices and girls wearing white veils and dresses once moved in procession through the church. The air sweetened with incense and the flowers displayed around the altar accompanied St. Thomas Aquinas' hymns as they echoed majestically through the domed chambers of the sanctuary. Such solemnity was only proper, for that was the way Corpus Christi was once celebrated.

Customs have changed since then. The processions and ancient pageantry are gone, but the Eucharist continues to hold its place at the very heart of Catholicism. A short excerpt from a sermon of Moses reminds us of the manna that sustained the chosen people in the desert. Even in times before Christ, God's people were fed and nourished by bread from heaven. Now, though, we partake of the true Bread of Life from heaven whenever we celebrate the Eucharist.

From the very beginning of the church, the meaning of *the* sacrifice offered by Christians was recognized. By eating and drinking the same Eucharistic bread and wine, a marvelous union was and is sealed both with the living Lord and with fellow-believers. Together, we are one single body, the church.

Jesus' words about the Eucharist are very familiar. Yet at one time, they were considered scandalous by some. That Jesus himself should be *in* any material bread and wine is certainly a mystery. When challenged about this, however, he spoke out even more uncompromisingly, "I am the bread of life.... If you do not eat the flesh of the Son of Man and drink his blood, you have no life in you. He who feeds on my flesh and drinks my blood, has eternal life,... For my flesh is real food, and my blood real drink."

The church has not changed her understanding about the Mass. Devoted sons and daughters still gather around the altar seeking nourishment and strength from the table of the Lord. None of us leaves this table hungry or thirsty. We are, instead, filled with the wonderful spiritual food and drink that satisfies the deepest longings of the human soul.

## COVENANT LOVE	1. Hosea 6:3-6
Tenth Sunday of the Year	2. Romans 4:18-25
	3. Matthew 9:9-13

HOSEA, the only non-Judean among the prophets, used words in ways that stir the heart. Noting that the practice of religion in his day had become a matter of meaningless words and routine acts, he declared, in God's name: "For it is love that I desire, not sacrifice, knowledge of God, rather than holocausts."

True love or *hesed*, as Hosea called it, is an outpouring of self, a personal commitment made to another. In Christianity, it is a covenant relationship between God and his people, one that calls for tenderness and affection along with mutual obligations.

Hosea's wife, Gomer, was an adulteress. She broke her marriage covenant vows to Hosea. Willing to forgive and start over, Hosea saw the prophetic significance of his own experience. Like Gomer, Israel had been unfaithful to the Lord by breaking her covenant commitment to him. But the Lord too was ready to forgive his capricious people.

In poignant words, Hosea prophesied, "Your piety is like a morning cloud." During the dry season, dawn often comes with clouds that seem to promise rain. But like the rains which never materialize, Israel's piety does not follow through.

Scripture says, "Without knowledge of God, the people perish." Without a deep, personal, intimate, and loving acknowledgment of God, life indeed becomes superficial and meaningless.

There is nothing automatic about God's grace. Like Abraham, we too must be open and receptive to it. God makes overtures to us, his children, but this does not mean that we automatically come to know, love, and see him. We must choose to receive him as well.

Matthew the tax collector began a new and exciting life when he responded wholeheartedly to Jesus' command, "Follow me." Jesus says those same words to each of us. They are an invitation to a wonderful, personal relationship with the Lord.

THE COVENANT FULFILLED

Eleventh Sunday of the Year

1. Exodus 19:2-6
2. Romans 5:6-11
3. Matthew 9:36—10:8

THE STORY of the Exodus is an epic tale about a ragtag band of people in search of liberty. After a heroic march through a desert, they came to Sinai, the mountain of destiny, where their flight to freedom was sealed in a covenant made with God.

As a rule, covenants were agreements made between equals. In cases involving non-equals, a *suzerainty covenant*, the stronger party would stipulate certain conditions to be met to insure the other party's carrying out of the agreement.

The Lord had already done marvelous things for the Israelites, carrying them through trials with one miracle after another. Even greater things were to come, however, if they listened to his voice and held fast to the covenant. Israel would be his people, a kingdom of priests, and a holy nation belonging to him, promised the Lord.

Such glowing words were well-suited both to the occasion and the noble setting of Sinai. This nation was to serve the God who had shown his love to them by signs and wonders. Thus would all nations learn of God's love. He would one day give the ultimate demonstration of his love by sending his only Son to die for us— sinners though we were. This is the essence of Paul's message to the Romans today—the good news of the new covenant sealed in Jesus' blood.

Full of such love and compassion, Jesus the Good Shepherd watches over his flock. Where many saw only the challenges in preaching the good news to the world, Jesus saw opportunity. He selected the Twelve and sent them out.

Jesus appointed Peter, Andrew, James, John, Philip and Bartholomew, Thomas, Matthew, another James, Thaddaeus, Simon the Zealot, and Judas Iscariot as his apostles. Armed with authority and power over evil spirits, they preached the good news that the reign of God was at hand.

Through the ages, the good news of God's covenantal love has reached us too. As a response, we serve him gratefully and with joy.

## TRIUMPH OVER EVIL	**1. Jeremiah 20:10-13**
Twelfth Sunday of the Year	**2. Romans 5:12-15**
	3. Matthew 10:26-33

THE PROPHET, Jeremiah, was an unpopular man who lived in hectic, turbulent times. Jerusalem was soon to be invaded by the Babylonians, and Jeremiah was a strong opponent of the prevailing but ineffectual resistance movement. When attacked for his stance, he prayed for vindication at the hands of his persecutors.

Such prayers testify to a passionate hunger for justice and righteousness. The defeat of all the evils that strike at the very foundations of human society is just cause for rejoicing, although we are always called to love the sinner even as we abhor the sin.

Sin and death trace back to Adam and his sin. The Second Adam, Jesus, cancelled the consequences caused by the first. As St. Paul wrote, "But the gift is not like the offense." Death entered the world by Adam's sin, but "much more did the grace of God and the gracious gift of the one man, Jesus Christ, abound for all." Sin abounded, but now grace abounds even more.

Jesus warned his disciples to expect active opposition, but also to not lose heart. Good would prevail. Neither a sparrow nor a single hair falls to the ground without God's knowledge. Those who stand up for the faith and its teachings may suffer persecution, but their reward would be great in heaven. Jesus himself will acknowledge them before his heavenly Father.

The cost of witnessing to the faith is high indeed. But if we are faithful to the end, we will see good triumph over evil and a glory that far outweighs the burdens of this present life.

GRATEFUL TO GOD

Thirteenth Sunday of the Year

1. 2 Kings 4:8-11, 14-16
2. Romans 6:3-4, 8-11
3. Matthew 10:37-42

FOR EVERY ACTION, it is said, there is a corresponding reaction. There is a kind of rhythm to human living, a natural, normal interplay between people. No human being can live alone and in isolation if he or she is to be really human.

Hospitality or sharing with others follows this law. Abraham entertained angels, and the prophet Elijah was made to feel welcome in a stranger's home. In both cases, the reaction to human kindness was, as seems natural, a blessing and reward.

Jesus brought to the world the good news that God loved the world. The response by those who believed was one of great joy, especially among the pagan peoples. When Jesus preached about the kingdom of God, great crowds listened hungrily to each word. Jesus did die on the cross, he did rise from the dead, and the gates of heaven were opened once more.

What is our reaction to God's great kindness? When being baptized, a believer is immersed in the waters (such was the ancient practice) as a sign of being buried with Christ. A Christian then rises from the baptismal waters, just as Christ rose from the tomb, marked and sealed forever as belonging to him. Now we the baptized share in Christ's divine and eternal life.

Our reaction to our baptism ought to be one of wonder and gratitude. Our ambition ought to be to grow closer to God and to do what we can to strengthen our awareness of and union with him. Our prayers should reflect our growing appreciation for the many good things he has done for us.

What we can do for God is to become his missionaries. We should be the bearers of God's Word in our home, neighborhood, and place of work. Even the smallest good works done in his name shall be given a reward. We can be sure that God's reward, in return, will be lavish.

A DIFFERENT KIND OF KING

Fourteenth Sunday of the Year

1. Zechariah 9:9-10
2. Romans 8:9, 11-13
3. Matthew 11:25-30

ONLY RARELY do we ever read about coronations of kings and queens anymore. On those memorable occasions, however, there is much jubilation, pomp, and circumstance. The marriage of Lady Diana Spencer to Prince Charles of England is perhaps the best modern-day illustration we have of such an occasion.

After Alexander the Great's conquest of the world, it became fashionable to imitate Grecian customs and ways of thought. Zechariah the prophet, however, rhapsodized instead over the Messiah, the Anointed One who was to come. He also would be a king, but not of the kind most people expected him to be. He would reign over a different kind of kingdom.

The kingdom Zechariah envisaged would be established without violence or war. Its king would be humble and unassuming. Instead of being a conquering warrior, he would come to bring universal peace.

After many years, in the fulfillment of time, God's only Son appeared. He came to establish the kingdom of God. Men and women set free from sin would become its citizens. In them the Spirit of God, the Spirit of Christ, would reside. They would be the very temples of God. Jesus himself would be the king ruling over all.

As his earthly ministry was ending, Jesus, the King of the Jews, entered the Holy City riding not a mighty steed but a humble donkey. This very fact indicated that God's kingdom would incorporate and value the lowly and the humble. Jesus was pleased that the Father had given all authority to him and that his mission was to reveal the Father to them.

There is nothing wrong with being learned and clever, but in God's eyes, the humble are esteemed because they are open to God and willing to listen. Jesus offers refreshment to the tired and weary. His servants must serve him because he is king, but the burdens he places on them are easily borne, for his "yoke is easy." The heavenly king's servants will know rest.

Jesus' followers are not spared trial and tribulation, but they are promised freedom from sin and the blessings of peace.

GOOD SOIL

Fifteenth Sunday of the Year

1. Isaiah 55:10-11
2. Romans 8:18-23
3. Matthew 13:1-23

RAIN, although sometimes seeming a nuisance, can spell the difference between feast and famine. When rain falls upon the dry ground, the enriched soil can produce a generous harvest. The Word of God is like rain. It falls upon human ears and enriches anyone who takes it in. Once received, it never returns void to God, but produces fruit and fulfills his purposes on earth.

Jesus often spoke in parables to clarify various aspects of his teaching about the kingdom of God. He would take a simple illustration from daily life and weave a story around it in such a way that his hearers were left asking themselves, "Is he trying to say something to me? Am I in that story somewhere?"

One parable Jesus told was about the sower and the seed. The seed strewn by the sower fell on different kinds of soil: on hardened paths, on rocky soil, weedy soil, or on good ground. The fate of the seed depended on how it was received by the soil.

When Jesus finished telling this parable, the question left in everybody's mind was "What kind of soil am I?" Jesus makes us face the question squarely!

Soil cannot control its nature or substance. But Jesus' hearers all have a free will, and thus can either choose to welcome or reject God's message. It is vitally important to be the kind of soil in which the Word of God will grow and bear fruit.

What we suffer in this life, St. Paul wrote, cannot be compared to the glory that lies ahead. We learn, unexpectedly, that the future of the created world is somehow linked with that of humanity. As a result of Adam's sin, all creation now "groans" as it is subject to futility and decay, yet it is not without hope. Nature is to share in the glory of the new order that is to come. God's plan is to be realized in a glorious return of all things to God.

PATIENCE AND FORBEARANCE

Sixteenth Sunday of the Year

1. Wisdom 12:13, 16-19
2. Romans 8:26-27
3. Matthew 13:24-43

HOW EASY it is for us to categorize others as either good or bad, instead of respecting our fellow humans as complex individuals with strengths and weaknesses! For example, how easily we fall into the trap of stereotyping street people merely on the basis of personal appearance. Tragically, this leads to snap judgments on our part which demean their dignity as our fellow humans.

But fortunately for us, God is patient and forbearing. In this Sunday's Old Testament reading, we hear about God's care for all. Although he is almighty, he is lenient, kind, and merciful to his people. He is quick to forgive us when we repent of our sins. By showing such patience and forbearance, God provides an example for us.

So too Jesus in his parable about the weeds and the wheat reminds us to be patient with our failing fellow humans. Our tendency, like that of the owner's slaves in the parable, can be to uproot anyone whom we suspect is bad, instead of waiting for God to separate the wheat and chaff at harvest time.

Fortunately, the owner demonstrates more patience and wisdom. He tells his slaves that if they pull up the weeds now, they might uproot the wheat as well. After all, only God fully knows why a person is apparently failing and what the final outcome will be. Only he is in a position to sit in judgment.

Paul reminds us that even though we may be weak and inclined to evil, in prayer we can turn to the Spirit, and he will address our deepest, inexpressible needs to God. Such humble and Spirit-filled prayer is a good antidote to a critical and judgmental spirit toward others.

DIVINE WISDOM

Seventeenth Sunday of the Year

1. 1 Kings 3:5, 7-12
2. Romans 8:28-30
3. Matthew 13:44-52

SOLOMON, the Son of David, ruled over Israel for forty years. This king's reputation for wisdom spread so far and wide that the famous Queen of Sheba decided one day to see for herself if he deserved such honor. She came specifically to ask him questions and test his wisdom. Solomon did not disappoint her.

There is a wisdom that comes from books, another kind that comes from experience, and still another that comes from God. Solomon's wisdom came from God. He was blessed with a compassionate heart, discerning judgment, and pure motives. He prayed only that he might be a good leader of God's people—able to discern right from wrong and good from evil. His prayer for increased wisdom was answered.

Divine wisdom is something special, for God would never make a mistake. St. Paul felt it worth noting that everything bears the stamp of divine wisdom. God brings good out of evil and cooperates with those who love him and are associated with his Son. Believers form with Christ a very special group that is dear to God. They are the church, God's dwelling place on earth.

Wisdom tells one to count the cost for any course of action taken. Is the pearl really worth more than anything else? The wise merchant thought so; he gave up all that he had to obtain it.

God's activity is a lot like fishing. A dragnet catches all fish without discretion: some good, others useless. But the fishermen do not stop their work to sort the fish then. There is wisdom in waiting. There will be time later to separate the good from the bad.

Jesus was making an important point through this illustration. God's kingdom is like the sea. In it, the good will mingle with the bad until the Judgment Day. On that Day, the final separation between all good and evil will take place. It might seem smart to sort things out sooner, but God has perfect wisdom in his timing of all things.

How can we be truly wise? One way is to value the things that God values. Our faith, for example, is more valuable than any pearl, and worth selling all to obtain. We also want to do everything as well as we can, for it shall one day be evaluated by God. Wisdom sees beyond the present to long-term, eternal consequences.

Finally, we must realize that our faith is not useless in the twentieth century. As every wise person knows, it is old yet ever new. Those who live by faith in these times shall be truly wise in the ways of God.

THE HEAVENLY BANQUET

Eighteenth Sunday of the Year

1. Isaiah 55:1-3
2. Romans 8:35, 37-39
3. Matthew 14:13-21

SOME OF OUR happiest memories may center around holiday meals and celebrative feasts that we have shared with our loved ones at home. Such times bond us together as a family in a special way.

Isaiah portrays God inviting anyone to his banquet who is hungry or thirsty. This heavenly banquet table will be filled to overflowing and free to all who come.

Life, however, consists of more than food, drink, fun, and friends. Isaiah knew that what everybody really hungered and thirsted for was God: the source of all goodness, beauty, and truth. God's invitation to the heavenly banquet is actually an invitation to enter into a covenant relationship with him.

Instead of just food and drink, God promises salvation, peace, freedom from sin, and deliverance from the archenemy, death.

St. Paul was carried away at the thought of God's wonderful gift. God sent his Son Jesus to be the Savior of anyone who would believe and receive him. He opened the gates to his kingdom to everyone. Absolutely nothing, neither height nor depth, nor anything else at all, can separate us from the love of God that comes to us through Christ Jesus our Lord.

Paul's hope is infectious. At the same time, however, we have to realize that although God's promises are absolutely trustworthy and that we do possess the promised salvation now, that salvation is still in its uncompleted form. The *full* reality awaits us in heaven. As long as we are here on earth, we live in a period of growth, ever deepening our relationship with God.

Jesus' magnetic words once drew a crowd of five thousand to an obscure and isolated place. Around mealtime, someone noticed that there was nothing to eat other than five loaves and a few fish. Jesus blessed and distributed the few loaves and fish, and as we know, multiplied the food miraculously. All present were fed until they could eat no more. What memories there must have been of that banquet!

In the Eucharist, we are able to partake of the messianic banquet now.

THE CHALLENGES OF LIFE

Nineteenth Sunday of the Year

1. 1 Kings 19:9, 11-13
2. Romans 9:1-5
3. Matthew 14:22-33

THE LIVES of saints remind us that we can make our own lives sublime. Many men and women have achieved greatness by facing the challenges of life one day at a time.

"It's a long road that has no turning," one proverb says of life. We live in an ever-changing world. We face many surprises, successes and failures, joys and sorrows. That's life.

Elijah had an unforgettable moment of triumph in his life when he faced the priests of Baal in a stupendous public showdown. His life was threatened by these enemies soon after, however, and he had to flee to the wilderness for safety.

On Mount Horeb, the Lord came to Elijah. Elijah first experienced a mighty wind, an earthquake, the crackling of fire, and then, in a still, small voice, the Lord. The Lord ordered his prophet to return home and continue his mission. The Lord dislikes unfinished business.

Paul knew conflict and persecution, but he had his better moments too. One of these came when he tried to describe the wonders of the Christian life, in Romans 8. But the Paul who soared high on eloquent wings was also a realist, his feet on the ground. How was he to explain Israel's rejection of the Messiah?

Whatever the answer, Paul was willing to die for his people. He saw a future belonging to God, and so, not without hope.

St. Peter is truly a great saint. He had often walked beside the Lord. But one day he heard the Lord commanding him to come to him across the stormy waters. He started out bravely enough. But he suddenly became frightened and began to sink. Jesus took him by the hand, and all was well. "Why did you falter?" Jesus exclaimed.

God is always available and present to those who call upon him in their hour of need. He is there for us when we too must face the challenges of the day.

JEW AND GENTILE

Twentieth Sunday of the Year

1. Isaiah 56:1, 6-7
2. Romans 11:13-15, 29-32
3. Matthew 15:21-28

PICTURE in your mind's eye a warm, airy room illumined by sunshine on a summer morning. The windows are wide open, inviting others to share in the warmth. In church we are in just such a place. Here are people of every nationality under the sun. Here no one is going to put us out because we do not belong. We have here no ghetto God, but the Lord of the universe himself.

The Israelites, returning to their homeland from exile, would have had to adjust to foreigners living there as well. Some of these aliens were God-fearing and God-seeking people who wanted to pray with them. They were people of integrity, eager to obey God's commandments and draw near to him by offering acceptable sacrifices as was the tradition.

How marvelous for us, this ancient vision of a time when doors and windows of ecumenism would be thrown open, acknowledging the universal lordship of God over all his sheep.

The entering of the pagans, or "Gentiles" as all non-Jews were called, into the church was not accidental, but part of God's plan from the beginning. In his love, even the Jews' "disobedience" became an occasion for good. Through their disobedience the whole world was able to enter into a covenant relationship with the God of Abraham, Isaac, and Jacob.

In Jesus' own time there were glimmerings of this dawn of ecumenism that was (and is still) to come. While spending some time in pagan territory, he performed a miracle in answer to the prayers of a Canaanite woman. Jesus cared about the Gentiles as well.

Today, thanks to Vatican II, we are privileged to see the windows and doors of the church opened to reveal the beauty and the depth of her faith. Jesus is Savior of all those who seek to find him. He invites anyone who believes to praise him with all God's children in his house of prayer. We are blessed indeed to be here in God's house through our Catholic faith.

THE KEYS OF THE KINGDOM

Twenty-first Sunday of the Year

1. Isaiah 22:15, 19-23
2. Romans 11:33-36
3. Matthew 16:13-20

As a gesture of courtesy, important visitors are sometimes tendered the keys to a city. As a rule, keys are give only to trustworthy servants because they are symbols of delegated authority.

"Who do people say that the Son of Man is?" Jesus one day asked his disciples. He was given a "they say" answer, so he rephrased the question to "Who do you say that I am?" Peter replied: "You are the Messiah, the Son of the living God." It was a tremendous profession of faith, and Jesus was pleased with it. He blessed Peter, addressing him by his Aramaic name, "… you are Cephas, and on this rock I will build my church,… I will entrust to you the keys of the kingdom of heaven."

Peter was thus singled out to preside over a mysterious kingdom. He was not made the chairman of the board, for the kingdom of God is not a business. It is rather a moral reality, a spiritual union between members who accept Jesus' kingship and desire to follow his ways. Perhaps a simple way to think of God's kingdom is to think of his church here on earth.

God established his church as a visible and present reality in order to help us in our quest for holiness. It is difficult to lead a good life without the support of others who also seek to please God. Peter and his successors provide us with God-ordained guidance from other human beings. We are never alone and directionless like sheep without a shepherd.

The church has many facets to her. It is visible in its members, but also invisible in its spiritual realities. It is present, yet it presses toward the future. It is bounded by time and space, yet it is also universal, destined to fill the whole earth. The papacy came into existence with Jesus' words to Peter. We are more blessed than we can say. The Vicars of Christ, those successors of St. Peter, have used the keys well for our good.

THE HIGH COST OF BEING A LOVER OF GOD	1. Jeremiah 20:7-9
Twenty-second Sunday of the Year	2. Romans 12:1-2
	3. Matthew 16:21-27

As JEREMIAH the prophet found out, being a friend of God can be an unpopular role to have. He had been called by God to denounce his countrymen, to rebuke their ways, and to warn them of the coming wrath of God. He was warned not to expect much appreciation or approval from his fellow Jews as a response.

Jeremiah was reluctant to open his mouth, but a fire began to burn so fiercely within him that he was driven repeatedly to fulfill his difficult task.

As he preached the good news to the Gentiles, St. Paul likewise faced frustration, opposition, and accusation. It was easy to receive the free gift of love and forgiveness from God, but there were the other aspects of being a Christian which were more challenging to embrace. They required a willing, patient, and enduring acceptance of the trials and sacrifices that come from bearing Jesus' name. St. Paul, did, however, faithfully embrace both kinds of privileges of being called Christian.

"... offer your bodies as a living sacrifice holy and acceptable to God,... Do not conform yourselves to this age,..." wrote St. Paul. He was not ashamed to share this high call of faith and love with believers living in Rome, even though it was the center of the pagan world.

St. Peter was praised by Jesus for having recognized him as the Messiah, the Son of the Living God. He was also rebuked by Jesus soon after. When Jesus spoke next about the death he was to suffer in Jerusalem, Peter took him aside to dissuade him from such a course. For this he was publicly and severely reprimanded by the Master, "You are not judging by God's standards, but by man's."

A protecting love does not keep a knight in his castle, but sends him forth to do great deeds. Our love for God may not make life easy, but it brings great fulfillment and meaning to our lives. As Christians we must be ready to walk bravely in the footsteps of our Master, willing to lose even our lives for his sake. The most important thing we can do in this life is to be responsive to God's love and accept his plan for our lives.

TAKING A STAND
Twenty-third Sunday of the Year

1. Ezekiel 33:7-9
2. Romans 13:8-10
3. Matthew 18:15-20

WHILE other people slept, sentinels used to stand guard over the city. If danger threatened, they would sound the alarm and the invaders would be driven off.

We do not face such immediate attack in modern-day America, but each of us is under a more subtle spiritual attack. Enemy voices try and persuade us that sin is not sin at all, or that we deserve to be happy, or even that there is no such thing as absolute right and wrong. They point out what everybody else is doing to breed discontent, as if numbers were the decisive factor for what's right and wrong in life. Thank God that we have a siren in our hearts, the Holy Spirit, to warn us of such enemy attacks!

Ezekiel the prophet, a true sentinel, sought to arouse his people from their dream world. Their exile and slavery in a foreign land was not due to the sins of their parents, or even to the sins of their enemies primarily, but to their *own* transgressions. They were reaping the consequences of their disobedience to God's ways.

Paul was not afraid to speak out against the sins of his day. He reminded the Romans of sins they should avoid: adultery, murder, theft, and envy. The price one pays for sinning is high. Avoid going into debt, he also counselled. "Owe no debt to anyone except the debt that binds us to love one another." We are never free from our Christian obligation to love all others. Each day we pay the debt of love. Instead of being impoverished by this, we discover that we are profoundly enriched. This is the positive and life-giving side of Paul's call to avoid sin.

Christian virtues are so rarely promoted or demonstrated that some might think living a true Christian life is virtually impossible. Only the most blatant sins are wrong and to be avoided, like the kind Jesus warns against in today's Gospel. Such virtues as honesty, self-control, purity, fidelity, and selfless love are assumed to be beyond our reach. This is not so, but we can only convict or persuade others of this by the choices we make in our own lives.

We must always be alert, ready to resist evil and fight for goodness. By doing this, we may be able to help others to choose the path of life too.

MERCY OVER JUDGMENT

Twenty-fourth Sunday of the Year

1. Sirach 27:30—28:7
2. Romans 14:7-9
3. Matthew 18:21-35

ANGER IS a very natural reaction to evil. It can be a protective instinct, alerting us to danger and calling us to action. In such cases anger is helpful and even commendable.

We read much nowadays, however, about people who go through life simmering with anger. Psychiatrists are certainly familiar with such people who spend their time and energy nursing grudges and dreaming of getting even.

In ancient times, a real man tolerated no nonsense. No one could step on his toes and get away with it. A swift and merciless reprisal would quickly follow.

Justice is essential, but without mercy it can easily be harsh and unbalanced. The Bible repeatedly urges the use of mercy in our judgments of others. Mercy triumphs over judgment. The great revelation about God is that the Lord is kind and merciful.

St. Paul made it clear that we are not the ultimate judge of others, nor do we determine their life and death. Jesus, who rose from the dead and is now seated on high, is the Lord of both the living and the dead. He, the great Judge, is merciful, so who are we to stand in judgment of others? We should be like our Lord.

Certainly if the Lord had not been merciful toward us, we would have died in our sins. And justly so. We *all* deserved death and eternal punishment for our sinful ways. We should regularly pray, "Forgive us our trespasses, as we forgive those who trespass against us." As we remember God's mercy toward us, we will find it easier to show mercy toward others.

Jesus teaches us this lesson in the parable of the unmerciful servant. This servant, forgiven a huge debt by his master, nevertheless went into a rage over a tiny sum owed him by another. He had forgotten the mercy that had been shown him. A servant forgiven by his master ought to be merciful toward others.

There are times when anger is called for, but do we choose the right times? Do we get angry enough at the right things? Do we reject with righteous anger all invitations to sin? Does our anger translate into positive action against crimes like abortion, corruption in government, or clear social injustices? There are times when it's appropriate, even our duty, to be angry. More often, however, our duty is to forgive and extend mercy.

GOD'S WAYS ARE HIGHER

Twenty-fifth Sunday of the Year

1. Isaiah 55:6-9
2. Philippians 1:20-24, 27
3. Matthew 20:1-16

ISRAEL'S exodus from Egypt was a memorable event in more ways than one. God not only demonstrated his awesome power in signs and miracles, but he also revealed himself to be compassionate and merciful, slow to anger and abounding in love.

God is also surprising and mysterious. The Bible brings this theme back to us time and again, noting that God's ways are not our ways, nor his thoughts our thoughts.

The psalmist said it well in Psalm 77:20: "Through the sea was your way,/ and your path through the deep waters,/ though your footsteps were not seen./ You led your people like a flock/ under the care of Moses and Aaron."

The thoughts of travelers often turn toward home. St. Paul spoke for many when he described his ambivalent feelings about his missionary life. It would be so nice to be home with God in heaven, but the needs of the church were pressing. Paul did, of course, choose to stay alive in the body so as to take care of the urgent needs of the church.

Paul was not the only one who knew that God cannot be out-done in generosity. Jesus' parables profoundly touched those lis-teners who had the ears to hear. Today's parable, for example, turns upside down any concept of one's just reward. Like the owner of the vineyard, God delights in distributing his graces and gifts not according to what is deserved, but according to his infi-nite mercy and goodness. He gives to *each* of us far more than we deserve. Our response is simply to use those gifts well and be good workers in the vineyard of the Lord. Thus our God is never far away from us as long as we seek him. He is always near, work-ing his will and purposes in his own way.

OBEDIENCE UNTO THE LORD

Twenty-sixth Sunday of the Year

1. Ezekiel 18:25-28
2. Philippians 2:1-11
3. Matthew 21:28-32

THE KEY to being successful in God's kingdom is lifelong obedi-ence and faithfulness. It doesn't matter so much what we say as what we do. Jesus, Paul, and Ezekiel all knew the importance of this lesson.

In Ezekiel's case, he pointed out to his fellow Jews in exile that a virtuous person must remain obedient and faithful throughout his or her life. Likewise, a wicked person in this life always has the opportunity to turn back to God and receive forgiveness. Our actions do count, and we are personally responsible before the Lord for how we conduct ourselves.

In his letter to the Philippians, the apostle Paul presents Jesus as the perfect model of such lifelong faithfulness and obedience. Paul also emphasizes that because of Jesus' faithfulness and obedience, even to death on a cross, God the Father exalted him as Lord and King over all. Jesus, our model, shows us the incredible fruits of being faithful and persevering as his humble servants. For, if we persevere, we too shall be raised up to reign with him forever.

The Gospel reinforces this same lesson. Jesus shares the parable of the two sons who are asked to work in the vineyard by their father. One promises to go work in the vineyard but does not. The other refuses to obey his father but later regrets it and goes to the vineyard to work. In the form of a rhetorical question addressed to the scribes and the Pharisees who are in his audience, Jesus makes clear that it is the second son who is faithful—in spite of his momentary lapse into disobedience.

The Master intended this parable for the religious establishment of his day which only paid lip service to the law. He is calling them to open their eyes to the real gospel values of fidelity and commitment, instead of external form and ritual. We would do well to heed Jesus' message also.

GOD'S VINEYARD

Twenty-seventh Sunday of the Year

1. Isaiah 5:1-7
2. Philippians 4:6-9
3. Matthew 21:33-43

PEOPLE travel great distances to visit the famous gardens that bejewel the land and delight the eye. Gardens in Paris, Vienna, and even our own Tampa Bay, Florida, boast of oases of color and beauty.

Isaiah the prophet once sang a song about a special kind of garden, a vineyard. The vineyard was designed specially to produce a rich harvest of grapes. In its center stood a watchtower to guard against trespassers. A hedge surrounded the borders to insure undisturbed growth. A wine press awaited the harvest.

The harvest, however, was disappointing. The grapes, instead of being sweet, were sour. The owner, upset with the results, thought of giving up on the vineyard.

Isaiah was not, of course, really concerned about some garden project, but about his own people, the Israelites. This vineyard represented God's people who had produced sour fruit, the fruit of violence and injustice.

Jesus used similar imagery in his parable of the wicked tenants of the vineyard. Even though the vineyard was owned by God, the tenants not only failed in being good stewards of the fruit, but they even beat and killed the owner's son for their own gain. This son of the owner was, of course, Jesus. This parable foretold the coming death of Jesus at the hands of wicked men. In God's vineyard, however, the ultimate fruit of the tragic death of his Son was still good: eternal life and salvation for the world.

Vineyards have to be tended well until the Master returns. St. Paul might ask us the interesting question, "What kind of vineyard are you?" The Master has blessed us abundantly and we ought, therefore, to bear the good fruit he has planted in us.

We can do that by following Paul's advice to the Philippians. The Philippians were among Paul's first European converts, and he had a special affection for them. Paul urged them to pray constantly and to keep their minds fixed on the pure thoughts of love and honor. If they were to do this, he said, they would know the peace of God which surpasses all understanding.

The Philippians must have listened carefully to Paul's words, for they were among the first fruits of the nations in early Christendom. We too will bear fruit as we love and serve the Lord.

PREPARATIONS FOR THE PARTY

Twenty-eighth Sunday of the Year

1. Isaiah 25:6-10
2. Philippians 4:12-14, 19-20
3. Matthew 22:1-14

IT HAPPPENS every time someone says, "Let's have a party!" Faces light up and eyes sparkle. Parties are something pleasant to look forward to and to enjoy.

In the first reading, we have a delightful description of a party, the banquet of God to be held on Mount Zion at the end of time. This heavenly banquet will be a victory celebration to be enjoyed by us forever.

Some of the prophets of old did not see the Last Day as such. They kept talking about doomsday, the Day of the Lord, as a day of wrath when the Lord would mete out all appropriate punishment to evildoers. This is true, but it's only part of the story! For those of us who have received God's forgiveness and walk in his ways, we can look forward to the party that will end all parties. Among the invited will be those who, like the Philippians who supported Paul, were faithful to God's many laborers of the gospel.

Today we also have a parable about a marriage feast. The king sent some of his faithful servants to call those invited to the party. Some of those guests, however, chose to reject God. Some rejected his invitation outright, others trifled with God by not taking his invitation seriously. One showed up at the party, but with the wrong clothes on—clothes that were inappropriate for the king's guests to be wearing.

There is a clear exhortation, even warning, here for us to take seriously. It would be terrible to miss a party given by God. We want to gratefully accept the invitation to God's heavenly banquet by receiving him into our hearts fully now. We also want to get ready for the party by wearing the wedding garment of righteous deeds. We want to be recognized and received by the host of the party when that joyous time comes!

GOD OR CAESAR?

Twenty-ninth Sunday of the Year

1. Isaiah 45:1, 4-6
2. 1 Thessalonians 1:1-5
3. Matthew 22:15-21

RELATIVELY few names of the great men and women of history have actually come down to us. Cyrus the Great, however, is one of these. He was once monarch of what is now Iran. He lived in about 550 B.C. He is remembered for his famous Persian palace, but even more for his decision to allow captive peoples to return to their homelands. They were even allowed to return with their gods and religious articles. The Jews were able to return to Israel with the precious furnishings of their temple.

Isaiah prophesied about Cyrus as the unwitting instrument of God for the delivery of Israel from her bonds of slavery. Cyrus may have been a great ruler, but he was still subject to the hand of God and *his* ultimate purposes for humanity. God is sovereign over all sovereigns.

Jesus of Nazareth lived a humble life, but he was soon thrust into the public eye because of his authoritative teachings and the miracles he performed. He healed many sick people and even raised the dead to life. Even nature, the winds and the restless sea, obeyed instantly at his word.

Jesus' preaching eventually got him into trouble with the ruling class. He continually preached about a spiritual kingdom wherein God's will was supreme. Jesus denounced external observances, which were either for show or for burdening the common masses, and called instead for hearts truly dedicated to God.

Although many people wanted to hear Jesus' political views in a time when a Jewish revolt against Rome seemed favorable, Jesus was silent on such issues. One day, however, Jesus' enemies confronted him with a political controversy: was one to pay taxes to Caesar or not? In other words, was Caesar more important than God's chosen people and their nation under God? Jesus replied, "Then give to Caesar what is Caesar's, but give to God what is God's."

Some scholars consider Jesus' response as the foundation for the co-existence of two legitimate but overlapping authorities—church and state—in society.

However, the apostolic church, characterized by its faith, hope, and love, has always maintained, "It is better to obey God than man." Be good citizens under Caesar, but remember that God must always come first in your heart.

THE THREE L'S

Thirtieth Sunday of the Year

1. Exodus 22:20-26
2. 1 Thessalonians 1:5-10
3. Matthew 22:34-40

WE, as Christians, live our lives within the boundaries of the three L's: liberty, law, and love.

Slavery was so common in the ancient world that freedom seemed the privilege of only a chosen few. For many in twentieth-century America, freedom means being able to do whatever we feel like doing. This, we know, would really lead to anarchy. Liberty for us is the freedom we have in Christ from sin and death.

When people form communities, they enact laws to promote and protect the common good. Laws are necessary for social order. Sometimes, however, laws can become an end in themselves. Keeping the law becomes more important than the purposes for which laws are made in the first place. Following laws then becomes legalism.

Jesus denounced this type of legalism whenever he encountered it during his public ministry. He asked instead that genuine love of God and of neighbor be the priority in men's and women's hearts. In fact, Jesus said, "On these two commandments the whole law is based,..." In other words, without love, the law was not being fulfilled at all. To follow rules without love missed the whole point of having a law in the first place.

The third "L," then, stands for Christian love. It is the response we make when God's own love has been poured out into our hearts. The law and love go hand in hand. The letter of the law kills, but the spirit of the law—to love—brings life.

May we live by the law in such a way that it brings life to us as well as to others. Then we will know what true liberty is.

THE HAZARDS OF RELIGION

Thirty-first Sunday of the Year

1. Malachi 1:14-2:2, 8-10
2. 1 Thessalonians 2:7-9, 13
3. Matthew 23:1-12

WE LIVE not in an ideal world peopled by saints but in one that has its share of time-servers and hypocrites. When such people occupy places of importance, it behooves their critics to be careful.

Malachi, meaning "my messenger," wrote under an assumed name when he denounced the religious practices of his day. In a later vision of the messianic era, however, he saw that a perfect sacrifice would be offered to God, in every place and nation, from the rising of the sun to its setting. Each Mass offered in our churches is that perfect sacrifice.

Like Malachi, St. Paul stressed the need to live by the Word of God without hypocrisy. He demonstrated that call with the example of his own life. He was a sincere, hardworking, gentle, and self-giving apostle, eager to share the Good News. He was everything a good priest should be. But the power of God's Word does not rest upon the man who proclaims it; it has its own power.

In Jesus' day, many Pharisees were men of high principle, although some were exhibitionists, sporting long tassels on their cloaks and conspicuous phylacteries on their foreheads and arms. (These little boxes contained quotations from the Law of Moses, who had commanded his people to keep the law ever before their eyes and close to their hearts.) Jesus again and again stressed the importance of a believer's inner attitude towards God. When this is genuine, it will normally and spontaneously find expression in external religious acts and good works.

Jesus denounced pride and the love of power. He spoke out vigorously against the desire to be held in high esteem because of professional or even religious titles. But any title that testifies to ability, competence, and dedication to the service of God and neighbor detracts nothing from God. Such titles are certificates that open doors to the service of others. "Whoever exalts himself shall be humbled, but whoever humbles himself shall be exalted."

TRUE KNOWLEDGE

Thirty-second Sunday of the Year

1. Wisdom 6:12-16
2. 1 Thessalonians 4:13-18
3. Matthew 25:1-13

OUR educational system has been severely criticized because many students are graduating from high school lacking basic skills. One shocking statistic states that one out of every five adults in America cannot even read or write.

The Bible speaks of another kind of ignorance: the absence of wisdom, without which we cannot graduate from the Christian school of life. Actually wisdom is a special kind of knowledge, gained, the Bible says, by insight into God's heart and just plain old time and experience!

Faith is a kind of wisdom, a gracious gift given by God to help us understand and properly evaluate the complexities of human existence. Faith is a kind of spiritual sixth-sense, by which life and death are appreciated as mysteries associated with a loving God. It gives meaning and perspective to our limited human minds.

Faith enables us to accept life as part of a divine process, not just as an end in itself, but the prelude to another better and longer life with God. Death too is part of this process. It is the gateway to that other life to come.

Today's parable deals with two classes of people. One class consists of Christian illiterates, those who lack basic skills to cope with important, real-life circumstances. Indeed, when an important crisis arose, these fools were not prepared and suffered eternal consequences for it!

On the other hand, there were the wise ones who knew what to do when the time came. Jesus wants us to be like the wise maidens who have learned how to live life now, but are also well prepared for the life to come. This kind of knowledge is the most important.

FAITHFUL STEWARDS

Thirty-third Sunday of the Year

1. Proverbs 31:10-13, 19-20, 30-31
2. 1 Thessalonians 5:1-6
3. Matthew 25:14-30

ALL OF US are called to be faithful to various practical responsibilities that make up our daily life. It might involve caring for a growing family or managing a demanding business. Whatever our vocation or call, however, we are called to be good stewards of the talents that God has given us.

Holy women who were faithful to their call grace many a page in the Bible: Sarah, Leah and Rachel, Ruth, Judith, Esther, and others. Some wicked women also appear and are scolded by some of the prophets for their vanity and evil behavior.

The woman of Proverbs 31 was endowed with boundless energy and a generous heart. She is not praised for her charm or beauty, but for what she did. She demonstrated balance and good judgment, and her husband and children were proud of her. She accepted her vocation and lived it day by day.

At Thessalonica, St. Paul spoke about the Parousia or Second Coming of the Lord, then as now an intensely absorbing topic. Some of Paul's devoted followers were spending all their time to figure out the moment of its occurrence, and this prompted Paul to tell them to get on with the business of living. Until Jesus returned, God's children should keep busy performing works worthy of the light.

The parable just read has nothing to do with running a successful business but much to do with personal responsibility. God has entrusted his children with the spiritual gifts needed to lead good lives. The gifts of faith, hope, and love help keep us working for God's honor and glory.

Muscles and intellectual gifts develop with use, as parents, teachers, business people, athletes, and artists well know. It is important for us to realize our need to grow spiritually too. We do so by using the graces God gives us. The more intensely we exercise talents and abilities the stronger they become. The reward for serving God diligently and with energy is, "Well done! You are an industrious and reliable servant."

THE SHEPHERD KING

Christ the King

1. Ezekiel 34:11-12, 15-17
2. 1 Corinthians 15:20-26, 28
3. Matthew 25:31-46

WE KNOW of several famous kings, like King David or King Solomon, who have changed the course of history for God's people, but none can compare with Jesus Christ, whose kingship we celebrate today.

In very ancient times, kings likened themselves to shepherds leading their sheep to pasture. They are ever ready to protect the flock, yet tenderly seek out any stragglers. Jesus called himself the Good Shepherd, obviously making reference to the ancient analogy in the book of Ezekiel.

Few today have ever encountered a shepherd personally, but we are aware of our need for what a good shepherd offers: direction, protection, and tender loving care. The world knows poverty, hunger, neglect, sickness, violence, and injustice. We struggle against such things with limited success.

More critical than such social and political ills, however, is the problem of sin. The external tragedies only reflect the internal state of the human condition. Sin and death are the inevitable results of our fallenness.

Jesus, however, rose from the tomb, victorious over sin and death, and now lives, glorious and immortal. And, in the fullness of time, *everything* will be made subject to him and he will reign with the Father as King forever.

Jesus teaches us in today's parable how those in his kingdom should live while on earth. By having compassion on his less fortunate children—feeding the hungry, clothing the naked, giving to the poor—we are serving and loving the King himself.

The reward for such faithful service to our brothers and sisters in this world is nothing less than a place in the kingdom above where Jesus, the King of Kings, reigns forever and ever in glory.

Year B

Sunday Readings

ONE

Advent Season

PREPARATIONS FOR THE LORD
First Sunday of Advent

1. Isaiah 63:16-17, 19; 64:2-7
2. 1 Corinthians 1:3-9
3. Mark 13:33-37

ADVENT is a time for prayer, soberness, and reflection as we recall that this world is passing away. Our Lord will come again, but this time as king and judge to restore creation and rule forever. That is cause for great joy, but also sober reflection on the current state of our lives. For we know not the hour of his coming.

To offset the lethargy and gloom of his people, Isaiah the prophet urged them to think of God. Is not God our Father, he asked, and we his people? We are his creation, the clay which he formed into a chosen people. "... rend the heavens and come down," he prayed.

After thanking God for the Corinthians, who had welcomed the faith, Paul reminded them that, enriched as they were with the gifts of the Holy Spirit, they should live their faith. Let them remember that the Day of the Lord lay ahead.

Here again is a basic lesson of the Bible. This life on earth is not the only life we shall know. There will come a time when the earth and all in it will disappear. Ushering in the new life to come will be a day of reckoning. On that day, God's servants will be required to give an account of their stewardship while on earth.

Advent is not primarily a season of penance, although that is ever necessary, but rather one of preparation. We prepare for the Second Coming of the Lord even as we celebrate his first appearance on that bright and wonderful first Christmas day. We realize anew how fortunate we are to have the true faith. It assures us that a loving Father is caring for us both now and in the age to come.

WAITING IN HOPE

Second Sunday of Advent

1. Isaiah 40:1-5, 9-11
2. 2 Peter 3:8-14
3. Mark 1:1-8

IN THIS LIFE we spend a lot of time waiting. We wait for big things like job offers or doctor's reports. We wait for small things like the light to turn green or the cake to rise. As Christians we live here on earth in hope of another better life to come.

God's chosen people spent years in exile waiting for a word of forgiveness. How they must have rejoiced to hear Second-Isaiah's assurance that their time of punishment was soon to end; God was coming with comfort and provision.

A message of joy was proclaimed. A royal road to the Lord's city would be constructed across the desert. The God of infinite power would reveal himself as caring, gentle, and tender toward the weak. He was going to be God with his people, "Emmanuel."

At the end of time, on the great Day of the Lord, God will manifest himself yet again. Will it involve, as is popularly believed, a fiery big bang? Only the Father knows. While waiting, though, Christians should live holy lives with both a sober reverence and joyful expectancy.

Even heavenly signs can be ambiguous, but there was nothing ambiguous about John the Baptist. He knew his role. He was the precursor who, in the spirit of Elijah, was to proclaim the good news: the Messiah had come! It was a time for baptism and a turning away from sin.

Although John's coming was heralded, he made clear that one much greater was to come. The Messiah would be much more important than his servant. So great was he, in fact, that John felt unworthy to even be his servant.

John prepared the way for the Lord by baptizing people in the Jordan River. The Messiah, he said, would baptize in the Holy Spirit. Charismatics are familiar with this saying. Jesus sends the Holy Spirit like a flood upon his followers, giving them the supernatural strength and gifts needed to do God's work.

John the Baptist was faithful to his mission; he bore witness to the coming of Christ. While waiting for Jesus' Second Coming, we can do the same.

JESUS COMES	**1. Isaiah 61:1-2, 10-11**
Third Sunday of Advent	**2. 1 Thessalonians 5:16-24**
	3. John 1:6-8, 19-28

IN REPEATING the exultant words of Isaiah 61, Jesus was announcing both the beginning of the messianic era and the fulfillment of that prophecy. He was the Messiah—the Anointed One sent by God to preach good news to the lowly, liberty to captives, and sight to the blind.

A joyous spirit is appropriate for the Advent season. We prepare for Jesus' coming by imitating Mary, who rejoiced as she waited for the birth of her Son, Jesus, our Savior. He was to live for others, not for himself. Therein lies the joy of Advent. God's kingdom is for us, even while we are in this world.

The more we appreciate the scope and the miracle of God's plan, the more we thank him for the gift of faith. In prayer, we ask to be prepared spirit, soul, and body, for the coming again of our Lord Jesus Christ. We want to live in such a way now that he who is faithful will call us faithful on that great and glorious day.

We can learn much from John the Baptist. He burst on the scene like a blazing comet. Yet he realized that he was only the messenger, a PR man. He was not the light, but only a witness to the Light. As people are drawn to us because we shine with the light of Christ, we too can bear personal witness to the one true Light.

As we look forward to Christmas, now just a few days away, we ought to bear in mind too that John was never thinking of himself but of another. John felt himself unworthy even to untie the Messiah's sandals. His mission was significant and necessary, but he himself was not the focus. He always pointed the way to Jesus. John was a lamp; Jesus, the Light.

In the presence of genuine greatness, we become more aware of our lowliness. When Jesus enters our world, it is not a time for selfish thoughts, but rather a time to appreciate his graciousness in coming to us at all.

COMPANY IS COMING

Fourth Sunday of Advent

1. 2 Samuel 7:1-5, 8-11, 16
2. Romans 16:25-27
3. Luke 1:26-38

WE CAN ALL relate to the excitement and expectation that comes with moving into a new house and making it into a home for those we love. Imagine God's excitement at the prospect of establishing his own house among men and women, and then making it truly a home for his wayward children by sending his own Son to take possession of it.

At the beginning of his long reign, David wanted to build a worthy house for the Lord. He learned that the Lord had other plans; he was going to build a house of David instead. Later, it would become clearer why David's descendants would play a major part in God's future.

St. Paul wrote to the Romans about the mystery, hidden in God for all ages, that had been revealed in their own day. Now for the first time it was revealed that God's house was to be built up by— and the Good News of salvation extended to—pagans.

The pagans were to be brought to the obedience of faith. They would be taught to accept and follow the faith Paul preached, in obedience to God's laws and plans.

Mary was asked if she would be willing to house in her womb a divinely conceived Son. We can imagine her excitement and her eagerness as she awaited the birth of her Son! She had become the house of God and in that same moment the mother of the church.

We can learn from the Blessed Mother to be living, loving houses of God, so Jesus can make his home within us. As we prepare for the coming of our divine Savior from the house of David, we fill the house of our heart with acts of faith and love. He who is coming will reign over God's people forever.

TWO

Christmas Season

For Christmas, see Year A, page 23.

NOT HOLIER THAN THOU
Holy Family

1. Sirach 3:2-6, 12-14
2. Colossians 3:12-21
3. Luke 2:22-40

THE HOLY FAMILY consisted of Jesus, Mary, and Joseph. Although they were the chosen family of God, Mary and Joseph did not flaunt their status but went to the temple humbly to offer sacrifice after the birth of their Son. Notice the sacrifice is that of a poor couple who cannot afford a year-old lamb as a burnt offering and instead offer a pair of turtledoves or two young pigeons.

Further, notice how this chosen family does not escape great trial and suffering. Simeon, a holy man who frequented the temple, recognizes Jesus as the Messiah and foretells his passion. He also tells Mary that she will experience great suffering as well.

Not "holier than thou," the Holy Family is a flesh-and-blood family that we can respect and emulate. Mary and Joseph are not rich in the eyes of the world, but rich in the things of God. They humbly obey God's law. And they embrace God's will, even when it means also embracing the way of the cross.

In a similar vein, Sirach calls us to honor and respect our parents, even if they are suffering the infirmities of old age and their minds begin to fail. It is a timely message today with many living to a ripe old age and relying on the care and assistance of their children.

Following the same general theme of family life, the apostle Paul describes the dynamics of family life as one of love, respect, and self-sacrifice among spouses and one of obedience by children to their parents.

Here is a master blueprint for successful family relationships: a model family to emulate in the Holy Family, Paul's plan for family life, and the duty of caring for one's parents in their old age.

For Mary, Mother of God,
Second Sunday after Christmas,
and the Epiphany, see Year A, pages 25, 26, & 27.

REVEALED AS GOD'S SON

The Baptism of the Lord

1. Isaiah 42:1-4, 6-7
2. Acts 10:34-38
3. Mark 1:7-11

PROMISES of justice, righteousness, light, and freedom rekindled hope in a broken and oppressed people some three thousand years ago.

That was when Isaiah the prophet spoke about a mysterious servant, one chosen and delighted in by the Lord. Imbued with his spirit, this servant would quietly and humbly bring justice to the nations, light to the blind, and freedom from slavery. The world would become a different place to live in.

After the resurrection, Peter learned that God did indeed come to serve all nations. In a dream, one night God revealed that he is not an ethnic or local God, only interested in the Jews. He is Lord of anyone who would receive him. Luke, a Gentile himself, welcomed this startling revelation which was first clearly enunciated in the house of the pagan Cornelius.

Isaiah had prayed that the heavens be torn open so that the Just One might come down. Emmanuel was to be Spirit-filled. He in turn would fill both Jew and Gentile with that same Spirit. The Gospel accounts of Jesus' baptism resonate with these and other familiar Old Testament themes.

Jesus' baptism was the beginning of his public ministry. He had for years quietly grown in wisdom, age, and grace. Now he would enter actively into God's plan for the salvation of sinners. His baptism was the first visible proclamation of his identification with the human race as its Savior.

Jesus fully realized the nature of his mission and that the fulfillment of the Scriptures would be seen in his life. Yet he waited until the time was ripe before he acted on the Father's will.

We, from every tribe and every nation, rejoice at the obedience of Jesus who was revealed as God's own Son. Through our baptism we, too, now enter into that intimate relationship with God where we are free from sin and alive to God in the Holy Spirit.

THREE

Ordinary Time before Lent

HEARING HIS CALL

Second Sunday of the Year

1. 1 Samuel 3:3-10, 19
2. 1 Corinthians 6:13-15, 17-20
3. John 1:35-42

WE LIVE in the midst of a great cacophony of noise. What we choose to listen to is very important. Some of what we hear can give meaning to our lives, encourage us in our goals, or perhaps even be the very voice of God! Other noises are a distraction or temptation from living the life God has for us.

The Bible records instances of God calling people to do things for him. Abraham obeyed God's voice and left home to go on a long journey to the Promised Land. That was his vocation.

Samuel, one of the greatest prophets, heard God calling him as he slept. It took him some time to recognize God's voice. But when he did, he cried out "Speak, for your servant is listening." God then commissioned Samuel. His lifework was spelled out from that moment on.

When St. Paul was least expecting it, God spoke to him. God told Paul that he was to become a herald of the good news that God loved the world and had sent his own Son into it to save men and women. There was no mistaking his call. God had spoken to him and he had heard his voice. Paul needed to be sure he had heard the voice of God because not only did he change from persecuting Christians to being persecuted himself for his faith, but he also had to preach the hard truth to hostile and defensive audiences.

Paul often spoke of lifestyles or sins that would cut their perpetrators off from God. Fornication is specifically mentioned as a sin, and one that—however prevalent—defiles the sinner. A Christian's body is the temple of the Holy Spirit, meant to be pure and holy unto God. We are not our own. We "have been purchased, and at what a price!" Paul exhorted each believer to "glorify God in your body."

Today's Gospel recounts our Lord's own call to be the sacrificial Lamb of God and his naming of Peter. Whether commissioned by Jesus or God the Father, both the apostles and the holy prophets of old had to hear the call before they could act on it. Once they really heard the voice of God, they were able to endure all obstacles and forsake everything to follow him. God has also called us into a life with him. If we listen, he will show us what we are to do for his honor and glory.

SPIRITUAL BLESSINGS	1. Jonah 3:1-5, 10
Third Sunday of the Year	2. 1 Corinthians 7:29-31
	3. Mark 1:14-20

JONAH the prophet was pretty unhappy when the Lord called him to preach repentance to the people of Nineveh. He tried to avoid this assignment, but in the end did as he was told. To Jonah's surprise, the Ninevites did penance and were spared. Jonah learned, as we have, that God is merciful to sinners.

St. Paul told the Corinthians that the world was soon going to end. No need, then, for them to grow too attached to it! Christians ought to have higher priorities than the things of this world. We still live in the world, and there are blessings and pleasures in this world, but we need to be reminded regularly of the transitory nature of earthly life.

From the very beginning of his public ministry, Jesus preached a gospel of repentance. Many who heard repented and believed. First came the fishermen Simon, Andrew, James, and John. They left everything and followed him at once. Their calling was now to catch not fish but human souls.

Anybody who has ever caught a fish knows that when fish are drawn from the water, they quickly die. But the fish who were caught by Jesus and the apostles, people of every walk in life, would not die. They would, on the contrary, begin to live a new, wonderful life of power and love when they did penance and welcomed the good news into their hearts.

It is usually people who catch the fish, but the one big *Fish* reversed the process. The *Ichthus*, Jesus Christ, God's Son and our Savior, works in an ocean we call grace. He shares with his catches his very own mysterious life.

Jesus, Jonah, and Paul all teach us about penance, detachment from worldly things, and the unending life of grace in God. Let us thank God for his spiritual lessons and blessings today.

GOD'S WORD OF POWER

Fourth Sunday of the Year

1. Deuteronomy 18:15-20
2. 1 Corinthians 7:32-35
3. Mark 1:21-28

AMONG the great men and women of history, Jesus Christ is without equal. When he spoke two thousand years ago, people experienced a strange excitement. He spoke with unmistakable authority. "I say to you" were words often on his lips. Today centuries after his death, his words still revolutionize the world.

On Mount Sinai the Lord had promised to raise up a prophet like Moses to lead his people. This leader would speak the very words of God. He would also intercede for them before God. This messianic prophecy was fulfilled, of course, in Jesus Christ.

St. Paul, an ardent follower of Jesus, announced to the outside world that Jesus was going to return at the end of time. Because Jesus' return was imminent and life on earth was passing away, Paul exhorted Christians to live so as to please the Lord of *eternity*. Both in this life and in the age to come, we should give the Lord undivided devotion.

In recommending celibacy—a counsel, not a command—Paul was not devaluing marriage. He was simply emphasizing that even marriage, a blessing from God, must take second place to wholehearted love for God. In the end, nothing will be more important than the Lord's coming.

Jesus attended synagogue regularly. Once in Capernaum, he even did the preaching. His authority as he spoke impressed everybody. Even when he was suddenly interrupted by a man possessed by an evil spirit, he remained in command. The demon cried out in fear, and Jesus sharply rebuked the unclean spirit: "Be quiet!" Shrieking, the spirit went out of the man.

When God's Word enters into human history, evil takes flight; and love, justice, and peace prevail. His commandments are clear, and they are the words of eternal life.

GOD KNOWS AND CARES

Fifth Sunday of the Year

1. Job 7:1-4, 6-7
2. 1 Corinthians 9:16-19, 22-23
3. Mark 1:29-39

LIFE IS A mystery in many ways. All around us we see the wonders and beauty of nature. Yet pain and sorrow, sickness and death, seem also always before us. Why? It is a puzzling mix.

We turn to the Bible for help, and there learn of a fictional character named Job. Traditional belief had it that a human's goodness always resulted in success and prosperity. Job, however, a good and upright man, had all of his earthly goods, his family, and his health stripped from him in a short span of time. Not surprisingly, he was depressed, confused, and questioning of God. What was life for?

Job did not have the assurance as we now do, that there is a life after death—a time when the inequities of life shall all be rectified. That is why we Christians, who have our share of bad times, are still filled with hope. The story is not over yet for us. There is more to come, and the end is a happy one.

One thing God cannot be accused of is coddling his friends. St. Paul knew this well. He traveled extensively preaching the good news. For his faithfulness, he was laughed at, beaten, run out of town, shipwrecked, and became physically ill. Paul was also careful not to use the gospel for gain. He supported himself as a tentmaker while he conducted his missionary journeys. He had a tough life.

The key to understanding why we face the trials we do is to believe that God knows of our sufferings and that he cares. He is never far away, and he will work all things out for the good. The presence of troubles is, in fact, our opportunity to trust him, to call on him, and to go confidently on knowing we are working out our salvation.

It is instructive to see how Jesus himself dealt with the pain and suffering of humanity. He touched, loved, and healed all those he encountered with the power of God. He also took times alone with the Father. Jesus' solution was to turn to God for help and direction at all times.

It is true that God's ways are not our ways; they are better. So powerful is he that he can turn our troubles to good use. Trust him! God alone gives life meaning.

JESUS HEALS

Sixth Sunday of the Year

1. Leviticus 13:1-2, 44-46
2. 1 Corinthians 10:31—11:1
3. Mark 1:40-45

GOOD HEALTH is a blessing. Few of us manage to get through life without encountering doctors, dentists, and nurses through hospital stays and office visits. Television ads promise to cure headaches, stomachaches, toothaches, arthritic joints, or nasal congestion. And the list goes on and on. But real life is quite another story.

Cosmetic imperfections are another source of grief for modern men and women. Blemishes, blotches, boils, and pimples are a few of the concerns of our complexion-conscious society. Dermatologists are very busy (and wealthy) people.

In ancient times, people worried about different skin problems. And it was the priest who decided whether a person had some curable skin disease or genuine leprosy. Leprosy was a common, but tragic skin disease. The sight of a leper aroused instant fear and revulsion in others. Lepers were shunned and driven from towns. Jesus, however, showed no fear of them. Indeed, he always treated them with compassion and care.

Once Jesus touched a leper, saying, "Be cured!" Instantly, the leper was cured. Jesus told him to show himself to the priest, the one authorized to give him a clean bill of health. The news of this miraculous healing spread like wildfire. Jesus provided a physical and emotional healing for the leper when he cured him. He loved the leper and then he healed him.

Jesus was even more concerned about the dreadful consequences of spiritual affliction—sin, the leprosy of the soul. Sin brings spiritual chaos into our lives and is a kind of spiritual death within a living body. Serious sin destroys our relationship with God and deprives us of his friendship and grace. It also cancels out any and all merits acquired by good deeds.

How comforting to be able to hear again Jesus' words to the leper, "I will do it. Be cured." and apply it to our own lives. There is nothing trivial about sin. Only Jesus can cure us of our spiritual leprosy and restore us to health through his sacraments.

We cannot only receive Jesus' love, we can also learn to love as he did. As Paul wrote, we may imitate holy Christians as they have sought to imitate Christ.

TRIALS AND RESTORATION

Seventh Sunday of the Year

1. Isaiah 43:18-19, 21-22, 24-25
2. 2 Corinthians 1:18-22
3. Mark 2:1-12

HARD TIMES are, it seems, inevitable. History is pretty much a record of trials of every description. Even God's chosen people were not spared from trials. Nor are we.

The Babylonian Exile uprooted God's people from their homes for almost five decades. Prophets had seen it coming beforehand and knew it was divine punishment for the people's sins. During the painful exile, however, other prophets began to speak of *restoration*, of the return to the homeland. The Lord was going to forgive Israel its sins and remember them no more. The actual return symbolized the mercy of God to allow us to return to his grace.

So too St. Paul faced many challenges and accusations in his missionary work, along with other more perilous trials. A quick-witted man, Paul was accused of vacillating between yes and then no about visiting Corinth, but he defended his decision. Joined with and like Christ, he made an unswerving yes to God. Jesus fulfilled all God's promises, did everything God wished him to do. By doing God's work, Paul was also on course.

Many a prophet had declared that God forgave sins, but none of them claimed to have power over sins themselves. Only God has that power. Yet one day Jesus told a paralytic man, "My son, your sins are forgiven."

To show that his claim to such power was genuine, Jesus then commanded the paralytic to stand up and walk. The man did so. The miracle showed that Jesus indeed had divine power as he claimed.

Sins lead to the worst kind of trials because they are spiritual hardships that we impose on ourselves and could have been avoided. Like a malignant cancer or physical paralysis, sin immobilizes us from living a life of power and love.

Repentant sinners, however, can flee the bondage of sin by turning from their sins and confessing them. Through his human instruments, the priests, God who is ever-loving and merciful, restores his children to spiritual health. Through even the worst trials we could ever encounter or reap because of our sins, God provides a way out.

THE HEAVENLY BRIDEGROOM

Eighth Sunday of the Year

1. Hosea 2:16-17, 21-22
2. 2 Corinthians 3:1-6
3. Mark 2:18-22

AS A MAN of committed love, the prophet Hosea was deeply saddened by his wife's adulteries. As a man of God, Hosea turned to the Lord for help. As a man of imagination, he drew the analogy between God and his people and his own circumstance of being a bridegroom with a wayward bride.

Hosea spoke of a return to the desert, to those idyllic days when God and his people were truly committed to one another in a loving covenant as they marched together to the Promised Land. There the marriage vows would be renewed and Israel lavishly adorned with precious jewels and gifts as befits the bride of the Lord. There genuine goodness, love of the Lord, fidelity, and justice toward others would reign.

St. Paul encountered much opposition as he preached the good news. When challenged that he was not a legitimate preacher, he conceded that he had no written letters of recommendation. He did, however, have his Corinthian converts. They were the evidence that he was a qualified minister of the new covenant, for they were the work of the Holy Spirit, letters written on the tablets of his heart. Their faith was truly evidence of the power and anointing of God at work. A covenant relationship with God always manifests such life.

The Law of Moses prescribed fasting only once a year, on Yom Kippur, the Day of Expiation. Piety however had prompted some Jews to fast twice a week. When Jesus and his disciples did not do so, he was asked about it.

In reply Jesus likened himself to a bridegroom whose presence called for rejoicing. He also likened himself to the Messiah; these were messianic times, the appointed time for jubilation. Once the bridegroom had risen from the dead and left to be with the Father in heaven, there would be appropriate times for fasting.

In thus replying to a question about fasting, Jesus emphasized the need to appreciate the spirit of the gospel. The heart of the gospel is not bound up not within the letter but within the spirit of the law. That spirit is one of generous love for God and our neighbor.

FREEDOM UNDER THE LAW

Ninth Sunday of the Year

1. Deuteronomy 5:12-15
2. 2 Corinthians 4:6-11
3. Mark 2:23—3:6

THE TEN COMMANDMENTS are not suggestions, but laws. They tell us how to do good, and avoid evil. Human laws are not arbitrary regulations, for laws are based on reason. Their aim is to protect and further the common good. Without laws, decent human society is impossible.

God made us free. But freedom is not doing whatever you want, whenever you want. Freedom is being able to do what you ought to do without the bondage of sin and flesh to stop you. Good laws help us to do what we ought to do, and to achieve what is good for us and everyone else.

The third and longest commandment bids us to "keep holy the sabbath day." It is good to get away from the daily grind, to take time to pray, and to thank him for the good things he has given us.

In a striking passage, St. Paul describes himself as an earthen vessel filled with a great treasure—the good news. Although roughly handled, he was not broken nor disheartened, for in everything the hand of God was at work and the life of Jesus was being revealed.

Jesus refused to have the law rule him more than the Lord of the law. When religious leaders accused the apostles of breaking the Sabbath, Jesus drew attention to King David's eating the breads reserved for priests. David did this because his human need was greater than the law. Jesus pointed out, "The sabbath was made for man, not man for the sabbath."

Jesus never worked a miracle for mere show. On one occasion, however, he did deliberately draw attention to a man with a withered hand before he cured him. His point was that no law can rightfully forbid the doing of good on the Sabbath. Love triumphs over the law.

Civil and religious laws remind us of our obligations toward God and our neighbors. As long as they are subordinate to the Lord of the law, we freely and gratefully observe them.

FOUR

Lenten Season

For Ash Wednesday, see Year A, page 37.

SPIRITUAL TUNE-UP
First Sunday of Lent

1. **Genesis 9:8-15**
2. **1 Peter 3:18-22**
3. **Mark 1:12-15**

OUR health clubs are stocked with sleek, glistening machines which promise to make us strong and fit, full of vim, vigor, and vitality. Many Americans will pay thousands of dollars to get in shape. Yet our inner life—the condition of our soul—is more important than a trim figure and healthy body. The condition of our soul reveals the essence of who we are. More importantly, it is clearly what most concerns the Lord. Lent is perfectly designed for a spiritual tune-up!

Noah was laughed at for making preparations for times to come. Religious-minded people are often laughed at too. After his baptism and forty days of fasting, Jesus began his public ministry. Some of his first words were, "The reign of God is at hand! Reform your lives...." Jesus' "tune-up" program was not a popular one.

Yet his own body, offered once for all, satisfied and overcame the power of sin and death. The gates of heaven were permanently flung open to all who would receive him. Even those awaiting his coming in the abode of the dead would be beneficiaries of the good news of Jesus Christ!

The most natural response to the good news was to be baptized. All who were baptized in Christ were united to him in a glorious new way. As they were immersed in the waters, they were leaving behind their old lives as dead and buried. But just as he rose from the dead victorious and immortal, so too all Christians, cleansed from the stain of sin, arise to the new and mysterious life of grace and holiness.

Personal sanctity is not a guarantee against being tempted. It was a sinless Christ, tired and hungry from fasting and penance, that the devil came to tempt. So too does Satan try the saints, seeking to distract them from an ongoing life of holiness. For all his tactics, however, the Evil One is really weak and helpless in the face of the power of the Holy Spirit who lives in us. The devil is full of suggestions, but he can go no further.

We welcome Lent as a time to grow in holiness and reliance upon God. A tune-up of the soul brings *eternal* health to our bodies.

PREPARING FOR GLORY

Second Sunday of Lent

1. Genesis 22:1-2, 9-13, 15-18
2. Romans 8:31-34
3. Mark 9:2-10

How marvelous it must have been to have lived with Jesus. To have witnessed his amazing miracles of healing and to be personally associated with him would have been an inestimable privilege.

Jesus' reaction to his fame was often to go off by himself or with a few chosen disciples to pray. One day he led the disciples to Mount Tabor and was actually transfigured before their very eyes. What was the significance of such an extraordinary event?

This miracle was in fact a revelation of the glory hidden in Jesus' soul. In that moment of transfiguration, Jesus' true splendor shone forth. Why did the transfiguration occur at that particular time? Perhaps because his apostles needed some special reassurance. Jesus had repeatedly predicted his suffering and death. Bitter persecution and trials awaited his disciples as well.

The Lord provided some supernatural evidence to strengthen them for the times to come. The disciples grasped (although not immediately) the implications of what they had seen. God's adopted children would one day also share in the glory of their victorious, risen Master.

God gently urges his children to look, with spiritual eyes,

beyond the present moment to a more important age to come. Isaac was Abraham's precious son, born in his old age, the son of God's promise. Yet one day God commanded Abraham to offer this same Isaac up as a sacrifice on the altar. Bewildered and broken-hearted, Abraham nevertheless obeyed, trusting with supreme faith in the ultimate goodness of God.

Abraham's obedience reminds us that nothing is more important than believing in a loving God. More than any earthly father could love his child, God loves his children. He demonstrated this by sending his own Son to suffer and die for us.

During Lent, the church reminds us to look forward and prepare for the glory to come. We need to be reassured as we perform our little penances and endure our little trials that a loving God awaits us in heaven. By keeping our eyes fixed on Jesus, we too, like the apostles, will be strong in faith.

FOLLOWING GOD'S LAWS

Third Sunday of Lent

1. Exodus 20:1-17
2. 1 Corinthians 1:22-25
3. John 2:13-25

CIVILIZED people live by law and order. Without the rule of law, there can be no peace or stability. Laws are simply a reasonable and authoritative determination of what best promotes the common good. Laws govern even civil and religious activity.

The Ten Commandments are ten laws, not ten suggestions. They are rules of divine origin which promote God's values and limit the sinful actions of humanity. They call for individual responsibility and accountability. Civil leaders would be very happy if their citizens lived by the Ten Commandments.

Jesus summed up the Decalogue with two commandments. His followers were to love God and love their neighbors as themselves. Herein lies the very heart of our religion.

The way to love of God and neighbor is through Jesus Christ. It is not the wisdom of humankind or miraculous works that convince true believers to follow God. It is through the suffering, death, and resurrection of Jesus Christ that we know God. We preach, as Paul wrote, "Christ crucified" and Christ alone. We trust God's laws because he is so wise. God is so much wiser that even his foolishness is wiser than man's greatest wisdom!

Jesus' righteous anger flared one day when he saw God's temple used as a marketplace—it had become a den of thieves. He overturned tables and drove the money-changers away in order to cleanse the temple. When the Jews challenged his actions, he declared, "Destroy this temple, and in three days I will raise it up." That would be the sign they demanded of him—the raising up of his own body, the true temple of God.

These obscure words Jesus once spoke are brought to our attention in Lent. We understand them better now. We realize that we must love God and neighbor, honor him appropriately, and cleanse the temple. Like Jesus, we are now temples of God. By obeying God's laws and his ways, we will insure that our temple remains clean in his sight.

RETURN TO GOD
Fourth Sunday of Lent

1. 2 Chronicles 36:14-17, 19-23
2. Ephesians 2:4-10
3. John 3:14-21

HISTORY has often recorded the mistakes and failings of people. Many of their lapses were due to sin. We do not like the word sin because it holds us responsible for much of the misery in life that we could do without.

The Israelites endured seventy years of exile as punishment for their sins. Then unexpectedly, Cyrus, king of the Persians, issued a decree of liberation; the captive peoples in his domain were free to return to their homes and serve their God.

For the happy Jews, the return from captivity was described as the second Exodus. Once God's justice had been satisfied, he extended undeserved mercy and forgiveness. In the same way, God has extended mercy to us. As Paul put it, "But God, who is rich in mercy, because of the great love he had for us, even when we were dead in our transgressions, brought us to life with Christ,..."

Our relationship with God, however, is not a cheap gift in which God does everything and we do nothing but benefit from his generosity. Even though we are utterly incapable of obtaining or earning grace by our own efforts—grace is a pure gift—we do respond to God's grace by making use of the life and gifts he has given us. We use our free will to choose for a life devoted to the honor and glory of his name.

While in the desert, Moses raised up a serpent which, when looked upon, healed those Israelites who had been bitten by serpents. This was an obscure prophecy foretelling Jesus' death and the healing effects on all who would turn to him and away from sins.

Lent is a time for us to look upon the cross and once again choose the Son of God. It is a time to do penance for our sins and re-examine our relationship with God. No longer wandering and lost, we can return from the slavery into which our sins have driven us and be home, once again, with God.

THE NEW COVENANT

Fifth Sunday of Lent

1. Jeremiah 31:31-34
2. Hebrews 5:7-9
3. John 12:20-33

CONTRACTS are an important part of any business. They spell out in advance what is agreed upon by employer and employee and contain clauses covering any failure to fulfill these obligations. It is wise to have contracts with people who can be counted on.

Dealings with God are, in a sense, non-negotiable, for mere creatures cannot bargain with their Creator. God has initiated a number of partnerships or "covenants" with persons throughout history: Adam, Noah, Abraham, Moses, the prophets, and the Israelites.

The climax of Old Testament revelation came when Jeremiah prophesied that God was going to make a new and superior covenant, one that was different from all others in the past. This new covenant would be written on the tablets of the human heart. It would be a contract of the heart, based on an intimate, personal, loving knowledge of God. The terms called for serious commitment, loyalty, and obedience to his will. It would not be a burdensome commitment, but simply the natural response of a grateful recipient to a generous party.

Jesus gave his hearers a new way of looking at life and death.

morphosis resulting eventually in a bountiful harvest. Both parties of God's new covenant have to die in order to enter into the contract.

Jesus declared that a man had to hate his life in order to save it. In other words, one has to be willing to give up his earthly life to obtain life eternal. Convinced of this, Jesus proved it by dying for us all. "Once I am lifted up from earth," he said, "I shall draw all men to myself." Mysterious words, but prophetic for our own paths to life.

The Savior suffering and dying on the cross has kept his part of the covenant. We enter into that covenant by dying and being raised to new life. Like Jesus, we want to remain reliable servants, faithful to the covenant of God. Magnificent rewards await all who follow him faithfully.

THE SERVANT

Passion (Palm) Sunday

1. Isaiah 50:4-7
2. Philippians 2:6-11
3. Mark 14:1—15:47

ON FOUR different occasions, Second-Isaiah spoke of a servant of the Lord. In the third of these servant songs, the servant received the Lord's own words of encouragement.

Sharing the Lord's words with others does not guarantee honor and respect, as the servant learned from experience. Yet he did not waver in carrying out God's will. He accepted it all, his face set like flint. He persevered in his task, knowing that in the end he would be vindicated.

This mysterious servant intrigues the reader. Who was he? Was he perhaps a collective symbol, standing for the entire nation of Israel? Was he a famous prophet or king? Christianity has interpreted the servant to be the Lord Jesus Christ himself.

As we gaze upon the servant we feel this identification to be correct. Jesus who was divine, being in nature equal to God, "emptied himself" and took upon himself the appearance of a slave. He was bruised and smitten as a slave. How magnificent a condescension! We are baffled at the idea of such a deliberate acceptance of suffering.

St. Paul assured the Philippians that because Jesus was humble and obedient, even unto death, he was raised up by God and exalted on high as Jesus Christ the Lord. Lord is the divine name of God. Thus, Jesus, the incarnate Son, is acknowledged as divine by nature. His perfect love and obedience to the Father received the most exalted form of praise from God. We may follow his example.

In fulfillment of an ancient messianic prophecy, Jesus entered the city of Jerusalem in triumph. Yet even as he received the adulation of the crowds as the Anointed One, he was still the humble servant riding on a donkey rather than in a kingly procession. He knew that suffering, humiliation, and death awaited him. He entered into God's will for his life bravely, providing the world with the example of how to bear suffering with faith, hope, and love. Jesus the King of Kings and Lord of Lords was also the perfect servant of God. May we share in that nature and be faithful servants too.

For Holy Thursday and Good Friday
see Year A, pages 43 & 44.

FIVE

Easter Season

For Easter Sunday, see Year A, page 47.

LOVE, UNITY, AND PEACE
Second Sunday of Easter

1. Acts 4:32-35
2. 1 John 5:1-6
3. John 20:19-31

FROM its inception, the first Christian community was known for its unity, charity, and peace under fire.

One of the leaders of this community was a Cypriot named Barnabas. Selling his property, he gave all the proceeds to the apostles for the care of the poor. The church thus set a pattern for almsgiving from which it has never wavered.

This Christian expression of love for God and neighbor was not a decision imposed on the church by some mandatory ruling; it was the spontaneous response of hearts touched by the love of God and his generosity toward them. Freewill offerings were not a way of buying prestige in the Christian community, but were prompted by gratitude and faith in the teachings of Jesus.

In this glimpse of the church at work we marvel at its unity as well. Unity was the singular mark by which the church was to inspire the world around them. The world was never really conquered by the Roman legions, but it *was* injected with a vigorous new spirit by Christianity.

Christians view God's world through eyes of faith, their gaze fixed on the water and the blood that once flowed from Jesus' side. Christians recognize that they entered God's family by the waters of baptism and were freed from sin and death by the blood Jesus shed for them. They know too that they can count on the Spirit of Truth to guide them and the church throughout the ages.

One of Jesus' last words to his apostles after being resurrected was the command to carry the gospel to the world. Along with this, he conferred on them the power to forgive sin! Yes, in those last joyful, exhilarating moments, the apostles were firmly directed to think of sin and their power to forgive it. Peace with God and with one another was one of Jesus' foremost concerns for his body, the church.

In this Easter season we reflect once again on the love, unity, and gospel of peace that the Lord desires to see manifest in the church.

FOUNDATION OF OUR FAITH

Third Sunday of Easter

1. Acts 3:13-15, 17-19
2. 1 John 2:1-5
3. Luke 24:35-48

THE FIRST Christian sermons all revolved around the unfathomable but incontrovertible fact that Jesus, crucified and buried, had been raised to life after three days. His own apostles and many others became eyewitnesses to the fact.

In those early Christian sermons the reader can detect a clear tone of Christian charity. Peter noted that those who had put Jesus to death had not known what they were doing. They did not understand that the death of Jesus, the holy Son of God, was part of God's plan for the forgiveness of sins and salvation of the world.

Jesus had hinted at his coming death and resurrection. The Law of Moses, the Prophets, and the Psalms had spoken of him as God's servant, and he fulfilled those Scriptures by carrying out God's plan. Now our Advocate is in heaven, interceding for us at the right hand of God.

God's plan is indeed mysterious. We can be sure that we know and love God, John tells us, if we keep his commandments. Religion is serious business, more than empty words. As Peter says, it calls for repentance, a turning to God, and being faithful to the Master in an ongoing way. The first Christians heard those words and received it with joy. Now we who live so many centuries later share in that same happiness.

The story of salvation is full of surprises. Jesus joined his disciples that first Easter morning, despite the closed doors. Almost playfully, he proposed that they touch him to see if he was real and then asked for something to eat! Yes, Jesus was really alive. Even better, he continues to live and make his home inside us.

The miraculous story of those early church sermons is the same good news that we hear preached today in our liturgies. We build our lives on that foundation of faith that Jesus Christ died, was buried, and raised to new life.

SAFE IN GOD'S HANDS

Fourth Sunday of Easter

1. Acts 4:8-12
2. 1 John 3:1-2
3. John 10:11-18

SAFETY is a matter of serious national concern. The Federal Bureau of Investigation, the National Security Council, and the Central Intelligence Agency are just some of the agencies that have been set up to cope with attacks on our national security. We want to guarantee our safety and protection from any evil or dangerous forces.

It is naive to suppose that our problems are only physical and external. Psychiatrists and philosophers try to address significant life questions such as: What does life mean? What is the real purpose of living? Who am I? What happens after death? What is good or evil?

Salvation, a word often used in the Bible, refers to a state of spiritual well-being. It stands for something presently existing, yet not completely possessed—a gift that cannot be earned, yet something that has to be worked at. It means restoring and upholding a relationship with God that men and women relinquished at the beginning of time. It is the only safe place to be.

The resurrection instilled within the apostles and first believers the conviction that life and death had a purpose behind them, for good or for evil. Peter's bold and courageous words on Pentecost revealed his new understanding that this life made sense and even led to a greater, more glorious adventure to come.

In the name of the risen Savior, Peter also performed miraculous healings. He restored one cripple to perfect health. A wonderful new power was at work in him and in all who would believe. Jesus, once rejected by men and women, was now alive, triumphing over the grave and reigning forever. His children had nothing to fear from the world any longer. They might share in his sufferings for a little while, but they would also share in his eternal glory in the age to come. Now and in the future, they knew that they were safe in the hands of God.

Christianity holds many paradoxes. Jesus did more for his sheep by dying for them than by remaining alive. The door to salvation was thrown open to welcome all nations and people and tribes. Salvation is for all who hear and faithfully follow the voice of the Good Shepherd. He promises, in return, to care for and protect his flock. The safest place to be is in the will of the Lord.

BELONGING	1. Acts 9:26-31
Fifth Sunday of Easter	2. 1 John 3:18-24
	3. John 15:1-8

Do you feel like you fit in well in society, or are you more of a loner? Do you think of yourself as a winner or a loser? The answer is that as a Christian, you are on the inside track and you have a place among winners because you belong to an organization called the Roman Catholic church.

The church is not a business; it is not IBM, or General Motors, or any other big corporation. It is a spiritual union of people who share a belief that Jesus Christ is the incarnate Son of God and the Redeemer of the human race.

We belong to this church. It is part of God's plan that we share our faith with one another. St. Paul sought to spread the gospel to pagans as well. They too can come to know the faith we share together.

Paul learned, as we do in our turn, that God's messengers are not always welcomed. More than once he had to leave town for preaching the gospel.

Despite opposition, though, Christianity continued to spread like wildfire in the first century. The fruit of the Christian life attracted and challenged many non-believers. They saw people willing to help others in their needs, and willing to sacrifice their very lives because of their love for Jesus their Lord.

John the apostle stressed the importance of doing good. Actions done in love and truth are as important as preaching the gospel of love and truth. It is interesting that John the mystic should have been the one to stress strongly the need of good deeds. True spirituality involves living out the faith.

Jesus described himself as "the true vine." His followers are the branches, nourished and sustained by the vine. The branches belong to the vine. By remaining intimately attached to it, they will bear much fruit.

We meditate on a simple, yet profound truth today. As Christians, we belong to one another and are called the church. As followers of the Lord Jesus, we dwell in intimate union with him as a branch to its vine.

PASSING ON GOD'S LOVE

Sixth Sunday of Easter

1. Acts 10:25-26, 34-35, 44-48
2. 1 John 4:7-10
3. John 15:9-17

LIFE IS a constant process of interrelating and interacting. Without contact with others, we grow dull and listless, we wither on the vine. Going outside of ourselves is a matter of life to us as well as one of love for others.

In a visit to Cornelius' house, Peter declared to this non-Jewish family that "the man of any nation who fears God and acts uprightly, is acceptable to him." As Peter spoke, the Holy Spirit descended upon everyone present, and all began to speak in tongues. It was the Pentecost of the pagans.

God's message of salvation was never meant to be hushed up or limited to a few specific listeners. No, his Word is for all peoples. We, the church, are meant to share the good news with any outsider who will listen!

When the Beloved Disciple, St. John, spoke of Jesus, he invariably used spiritual metaphors such as "light," "life," and "truth." None of these analogies, however, is perhaps as penetrating or profound as his simple statement: "... God is love." Love identifies the essence of who God is. It is his nature to love. God so loved the world that he sent his Son to it as an offering for our sins.

It is sweet to know that another loves us. We are, as Jesus said, his friends. The love of friends is a special kind of love. It involves holding something in common, an unselfish spirit, and mutual commitment.

God shares his life with us, not because he has to, or because he needs to for his own sake, but simply because he wants to. Love is like that. it is going outside of oneself for the sake of another. As Jesus' friends, our response is simply to be as committed to him as he has already shown himself to be with us.

Today we show our love for God by rededicating ourselves to living out the faith daily, by passing it on to our children, by showing concern for the poor and the needy, and by sharing our faith with all who seek the freedom of the children of God. It is through us that the message, "God is love," can be passed on to enrich and delight our neighbors everywhere in the world.

THE GREAT COMMISSION

Ascension Thursday

1. Acts 1:1-11
2. Ephesians 1:17-23
3. Mark 16:15-20

THE GREAT Doctor of the Church, St. Augustine, considered today's feast the greatest of them all, for it marked Jesus' entrance into a new and glorious condition of being.

The ascension took place near the Garden of Gethsemane, toward Bethany. After blessing his disciples, Jesus was carried up into heaven. The "up" is not primarily spatial; it essentially means that Jesus entered into God's presence. A cloud received him out of the apostles' sight.

Mark tells us that Jesus appeared to the eleven and issued the great commission before ascending into heaven and taking his seat at the Father's right hand. Jesus told his apostles to preach the good news of salvation to the entire world, baptizing those who would believe in the gospel.

Moreover, Jesus describes how powerful signs will accompany the preaching of the gospel, confirming its power to save. Demons will be expelled in the name of Jesus. Believers will speak in entirely new languages. The sick will recover through the laying on of hands and prayer in Jesus' name. Here we see the power and authority of the risen and ascended Christ, who sends the Holy Spirit to empower believers who act in his name.

The risen and ascended Lord did take a glorified human body with him into heaven. His body was both an instrument of our redemption, and a testimony to our worth. In heaven Jesus wears it still. When Jesus comes again, he will appear in that same glorified humanity.

The ascension filled the apostles with great joy, for they were now convinced that the Master was divine. Soon to be baptized in the Spirit, they would then begin their mission of carrying the good news to the whole world and initiating all nations into the mystery of faith through baptism in water.

The ascension had also, as both Paul and Mark perceived, a cosmic dimension, for it spelled the overthrow of demonic powers. It was further proof that Jesus was ruler of all things and head over all.

St. Augustine was right. The feast of the ascension is a truly glorious feast, the crowning touch added to the death and resurrection of Jesus the Lord.

THE CHRISTIAN BOND

Seventh Sunday of Easter

1. Acts 1:15-17, 20-26
2. 1 John 4:11-16
3. John 17:11-19

PEOPLE are certainly not animals, but like animals they tend to congregate together. In groups there is strength. Much can be done when the skills and energies of like-minded people are pooled. In business, sports, hobbies, and politics, people who share a common interest often pool their resources, work together, and accomplish impressive feats.

In spiritual matters, too, natural groupings are important. The apostles had been chosen by Christ to carry out a common mission. They were to preach about the spiritual kingdom Jesus had come to establish on earth.

Even amidst their diversity, the unity of the apostles was significant and essential. The apostles were twelve in number, but they became one single corporate body, the church.

The secret to unity in the church lies in promoting love above all other interests. God is love and loves all his children. If he loves us all, so ought we to love and be able to love one another. True Christianity is to love God and to love our neighbor as ourselves.

In praying to his heavenly Father, Jesus asked that unity might prevail among the disciples. He did not ask that they be taken out of the world, but that they be kept safe from the Evil One, and that they be consecrated in truth.

Consecration makes its objects something special. What is consecrated is set apart and dedicated to God. As Jesus prepared himself for his sacrificial death on the cross, he prayed that his disciples might enter with faith into his sufferings, but also share in his triumph and eternal glory to come. To be thus bonded to Jesus is the ambition of every true disciple. Union with Christ and unity within his church is the call we may respond to today.

For Pentecost Sunday, see Year A, page 55.

SIX

Ordinary Time after Easter

OUR KNOWLEDGE OF GOD
AS HE IS

Trinity Sunday

1. Deuteronomy 4:32-34, 39-40
2. Romans 8:14-17
3. Matthew 28:16-20

THE MORE we see in this world, the more we marvel. It is a world full of beauty and creativity. It could not have happened by chance, but was surely the creation of a maker, the masterpiece of a great artist. If we believe this, then the natural question to ask is who is this maker? What is he like?

Science and reason can explain many things to us. But spiritual revelation can tell us even more. For example, it is spiritual knowledge that convinces us there is a God, that he cares about us personally, and that he has revealed himself as three persons who share the same divine nature.

Moses reminds us that God indeed created us and that he saves his people through personal interaction and divine protection. The New Testament, however, speaks of something even more amazing and miraculous. God came to earth personally to share in our humanity and to be the Savior of humanity. God allowed himself to become human, bound by space and time, in order to save us.

The God-Man, Jesus, then revealed another incredible truth. He and the Father were going to send the Holy Spirit, the Spirit of God, to dwell in us.

After his resurrection, Jesus visited his apostles. All power was now his, and he used it to commission them to make disciples of all the nations, baptizing them in the name of the Father, Son, and Holy Spirit.

Today we celebrate with the church universal the mystery of the Most Holy Trinity. Through this mystery, we know something about God as he is in himself. He is not a lonesome God; he is Three-in-One. He needs nothing to make him happy, yet he has created the universe for us. Sinless, he sent his Son to save us while we were yet sinners. Loving and good, he sends his Holy Spirit to sanctify us. Small wonder that we celebrate the Triune God today.

A SIGN OF UNITY

Body and Blood of Christ

1. Exodus 24:3-8
2. Hebrews 9:11-15
3. Mark 14:12-16, 22-26

TODAY we celebrate the great feast of unity. When there is unity within a family, nation, or even simply a business enterprise, great strength exists. There is a sense of belonging, a community of purpose, and a sharing of hearts.

All these things happen when we take religion seriously and lead good Christian lives. When we are faithful to one another, we are being faithful to our covenant with God. Covenants are definite agreements between people. These are a type of contract wherein each party promises to do certain things. Our relationship with God is a covenant. We promise to keep God's commandments, and he promises to be our God.

Jesus summarized the Ten Commandments in two more general ones that called us to love God and one another. By shedding his blood on the cross, he sealed this new covenant made for us. Through baptism we enter into that covenant and belong to a larger grouping of his people, the church. We are happy and proud to belong to it.

Under this umbrella, in this new covenant, we share in the great strength of Christ by making use of the sacraments, especially the sacrament of his Body and Blood. At the Last Supper, Jesus said, "This is my body.... This is my blood," and gave it to them to eat. He was their food, giving them spiritual life and strength.

The Eucharist is a great sign of unity. We believe that in it, Jesus is truly present, body and soul. We believe that by eating this heavenly food, we become one with him, sharing in his life and his strength, and his mission.

Jesus abides in our midst, not just as a sweet memory, but as a source of spiritual life now. He is the greatest sign, the great reminder of our covenant with God.

As God's people, we reaffirm our commitment to our covenant with him and with one another each time we receive Holy Communion.

ULTIMATE VICTORY

Tenth Sunday of the Year

1. Genesis 3:9-15
2. 2 Corinthians 4:13—5:1
3. Mark 3:20-35

BOTH ON television and in books, happy endings are still popular. The good guys always win after heroic struggles against the bad guys. Readers want to relate to the heroes and rejoice in the triumph of goodness over evil.

The Bible opens with a dramatic success story. Adam and Eve are led into sin by a wily serpent, the devil. Then God enters the scene. He obtains a grudging admission of failure from the two sinners who would rather place the blame on another. Then he announces his verdict. The Evil One is doomed to ultimate failure and humiliation for his actions. Through the woman's Son, God will be victorious. This is the first great messianic promise in the Bible.

In any contest, a positive attitude is a definite plus. In his turbulent missionary life, St. Paul's faith was so strong that he took all setbacks in stride. He knew that God's plan would ultimately be carried out and his glory revealed.

Yes, but when? and how? In today's wonderful passage, Paul concedes that though his body is fading away, his inner being, his spirit, is being renewed each day. He walks by faith, not by sight. He looks forward to the heavenly dwelling God will provide for him as a reward for his faith. This would happen in God's good time.

Jesus spearheaded the attack on Satan's kingdom. Yet he was maligned and even accused of being in league with the devil. "Can a house divided against itself still stand?" he responded. Would Satan help him defeat Satan? No, he was Satan's archenemy.

It is hard to imagine anyone refusing the gift of life Jesus came to offer. Yet the forces of evil amassed against Jesus persuaded many to oppose him and his divine mission. This decision to reject the Spirit would, Jesus said, rule out the very means of forgiveness.

Nothing meant more to Jesus than preaching the good news. In him and through him the human story would have a happy ending. All God's promises would be fulfilled as promised.

DREAMS THAT COME TRUE

Eleventh Sunday of the Year

1. Ezekiel 17:22-24
2. 2 Corinthians 5:6-10
3. Mark 4:26-34

THE WORLD is full of dreams and dreamers. We dream randomly at night. By day we dream about what we shall do with our lives. Dreams can motivate us and explain our persistence and courage against many obstacles.

As Christians, we do not set our sights too low as dreamers, for we are made only a little less than the angels. We have a powerful inner spiritual life. In our hopes, dreams, and ambitions, we must make room for the supreme reality of God at work in us and through us.

Ezekiel the prophet had a dream that stirred hope in his fellow exiles: God was to bring about a new beginning. A tiny shoot plucked from the crest of the lofty cedar, Babylon, would flourish on a high mountain, Jerusalem. The Lord was going to liberate and restore his people.

St. Paul dreamed of being with God in everlasting bliss. But he was still alive, at the time, willing to walk by faith, not by sight. No matter if the present situation was discouraging; on Judgment Day God would reward those who had been faithful.

The theme of waiting with certainty, which is hope, runs through the many parables Jesus preached about the kingdom of God. He used the seed sown by the farmer to illustrate what he was trying to teach them about the church and about life itself. A seed is sown in the ground. It takes root and grows in a mysterious fashion. When harvest time eventually comes, the sower reaps his crop.

Jesus also used the example of the tiny mustard seed. Insignificant, at first, it becomes a sizable shrub. The farmer plays a part in the process by planting and watering the seed, but the seed follows its own mysterious path of growth.

Jesus' personal dream was about the kingdom of God on earth. It too was destined for mysterious growth and a great future. In it, humanity's dreams of spiritual freedom and liberty would become reality. The wonderful thing, of course, is that such dreams do come true in Christ.

THE STORMS OF LIFE
Twelfth Sunday of the Year

1. Job 38:1, 8-11
2. 2 Corinthians 5:14-17
3. Mark 4:35-41

IN THE STORMS of life, we need spiritual vision to reach shore safely. That kind of vision is something only God can provide as Job, the apostle Paul, and the disciples discover in today's readings.

Why bad things happen to good people is indeed puzzling. Job was a good man, and in his suffering challenged God to explain. God answered "out of the storm," firing question after question at Job. Obviously, Job didn't know much about the sorts of issues God was raising. In the end, he conceded that suffering was among things "too wonderful for me."

Still, Job had raised a good point. Augustine and Thomas had an answer to the problem: God does not cause evil, but he permits it. He is so powerful that he can bring good out of evil. That answer stands. Suffering has a place in God's plan. But we need spiritual eyes to comprehend that truth.

Paul was a controversial figure, cheered and jeered and often thrown into jail. Nothing could slow him down. Jesus' death had shown God's love for the world; and Paul, driven by that love, returned it with all his strength. He was a man of spiritual vision.

The fact that Jesus rose from the dead puts him in a class apart, not to be judged by human standards. Anyone who is "in Christ" is a *new creation* and has only just begun to live! Nothing else, Paul argued, matters but the love of Christ.

Once while sailing, Jesus' boat was tossed about by a squall. The disciples were not unaccustomed to rough water, but apparently this time was different. They became frightened. Jesus had taken a seat in the stern and, tired out by a day of preaching, had fallen asleep. The disciples woke him up. In their fear, they asked him somewhat rudely if he knew they were going down.

Jesus calmly commanded the wind and the sea, "Quiet! Be still!" And he was obeyed. Then he asked simply, "Why were you afraid?" God is never unaware of our plight. In our pain, fright, and anxiety, we have only to turn confidently to him who loves us.

LORD OF LIFE	1. Wisdom 1:13-15; 2:23-24
Thirteenth Sunday of the Year	2. 2 Corinthians 8:7, 9, 13-15
	3. Mark 5:21-43

EVERY AGE produces its share of sages and philosophers who attempt to address some of life's big questions. Likewise, we have an abundance of doctors and psychiatrists, health spas and counseling clinics, to explain the various ailments of the human body and soul. Their very number indicates that we are recognizing the complexity of human beings. We are a combination of matter and soul, body and spirit, requiring a great deal of attention.

We have physical needs (food, clothing, shelter), and spiritual and emotional needs (love, understanding, purpose for living, relationship with God, moral codes). Death will terminate our physical existence, yet because we are born anew of the Spirit and made in God's image, we possess immortality of the soul. Divine wisdom tells us that we are destined for eternal life.

The apostle Paul understood the balance between physical and spiritual needs. He was not an unworldly visionary. He urged Christians to help fellow believers who were in trouble, not only with their prayers, but with their finances as well. Let them be generous givers. If we all share in our abundance, then in times of lack, those in need will surely be provided for.

Jesus knew, of course, that eternal life awaited believers, yet he understood and expressed loving concern for those still suffering from physical diseases and grief over death. He chose to personally comfort and heal while on earth.

When a sick woman in the crowd touched him, he knew she had done so, and used the occasion to both heal her and teach the crowds an important lesson. He cured the woman, but emphasized too that it was a reflection of her spiritual health (her faith) that her physical health was restored.

Jesus demonstrated his love and power again when he raised a little girl from the dead. Just as Jesus restored this girl's physical life, we thank God for the new spiritual life he has restored to us. Whether in the physical world or spiritual realm, Jesus reigns as Lord of life.

GOD'S CHOSEN SERVANTS

Fourteenth Sunday of the Year

1. Ezekiel 2:2-5
2. 2 Corinthians 12:7-10
3. Mark 6:1-6

GOD chose a priest in exile with the Israelites to be his mouthpiece to them. Ezekiel was a feisty character. He made it clear to this restless and stubborn people that he spoke in the Lord's name, and that a day of reckoning was coming when each sinner would have to answer for his or her own sins.

St. Paul was another servant of God called to speak some hard truths to God's people. To keep Paul humble, however, a "thorn in the flesh" afflicted him. God's answer to Paul's prayers for deliverance from the thorn was, "My grace is enough for you, for in weakness power reaches perfection." God's servants need not be perfect for them to be anointed and called by God for his works. This should be a comfort and encouragement to us!

In Nazareth, the perfect servant attended synagogue regularly. There Jesus read and preached with a clarity and force that aroused wonder among his hearers. "Where did he get all this?" they asked. "How is it such miraculous deeds are accomplished by his hands? Isn't this the carpenter, the son of Mary...?" They could not reconcile the humble carpenter with the Anointed One of God right in their midst.

The old proverb says: "Familiarity breeds contempt." Jesus knew this quite well, and sadly observed: "No prophet is without honor except in his native place,..." Because of their skepticism, Jesus was only able to work a few miracles in his hometown.

True preachers, pastors, and servants of God are not laboring for the praises of men and women or out of personal ambition. They are serving out of a desire to obey God's call on their lives. Today we may thank God and them for their service in God's kingdom.

GOD'S REFORMS

Fifteenth Sunday of the Year

1. **Amos 7:12-15**
2. **Ephesians 1:3-14**
3. **Mark 6:7-13**

CENTURIES ago, the sage Heraclitus said, "Everything is changing. Life flows like a river. No one can put his hand into the same spot in it twice." Some contemporary philosophers have a different view, however, saying the exact opposite, "Nothing changes. Change is an illusion."

The fact is that both views contain some truth. In some ways life is organic and dynamic. No moment of existence is ever repeated. On the other hand, some realities and truths in life don't change. "Nothing is new under the sun." Some changes, however, are good and even necessary, but the flow of life seems to run counter to any change.

Amos the prophet once ventured into Bethel, the religious seat of the Northern Kingdom. He lashed out against the luxurious lifestyle of king and priest, at the cost of the poor and needy.

Amos was all but bodily thrown out of the temple and town for his words. He had dared to criticize the *status quo*. He warned that when the Day of the Lord came, such sins would be justly punished.

The apostle Paul also believed in some changes in society. Many gladly received Paul's preaching that Jesus is Lord, but others resented his apparent attack on traditional Jewish life. As a result, Paul saw the inside of many a prison.

The doors of salvation, Paul held, were open to all men and women. Jesus' death for us all meant that God cared for Gentiles as well as Jews. United to Christ in baptism, they were now God's adopted children! This was such a radical change from traditional Jewish teaching, that it seemed too good to be true. Yet it is all true even today.

Jesus sent his disciples out to preach a message which is the same yesterday, today, and forever. It will never change, although it continues to be proclaimed in a world that is constantly changing. We ought to thank God for the church which is ever old, yet ever new. He, who transcends all generations and ages, will guard the church and the faith for eternity.

THE HEART OF A SHEPHERD

Sixteenth Sunday of the Year

1. Jeremiah 23:1-6
2. Ephesians 2:13-18
3. Mark 6:30-34

THOSE WHO lead God's people need the heart of a shepherd to pastor others effectively. Otherwise, the flock is quickly misled and scattered without direction and purpose. That was as true in Jeremiah's day as in the time of Jesus. And it is still true today.

In Jeremiah's day, the nation of Judah has just faced defeat and deportation because its kings have failed to tend the sheep. That is Jeremiah's assessment of the nation's sorry condition. But Jeremiah prophesies that one day a righteous king of the line of David shall govern God's people wisely. Then there will be peace and security.

On that new day, God himself will "gather the remnant of [his] flock" and raise up shepherds who will care for his sheep, instead of pursuing their own selfish ends. Further, there is the promise that the sheep shall prosper and multiply in lush, green meadows under this new order.

In Mark's Gospel, we see Jesus caring for the scattered and divided flock of his own day as the Good Shepherd. He has just gone off to a deserted place with the apostles. But he and the apostles are spotted leaving in a boat, and a multitude pursues them on foot.

Rather than sending them away, Jesus has compassion on the crowd and begins to teach them. As the Good Shepherd, he is feeding and instructing his flock.

Paul tells us that because this Good Shepherd laid down his life through the shedding of his blood, God's people have been given "access in one Spirit to the Father." Now this one flock even includes Gentile believers who could not become members of God's people because of the law of the old covenant. Thus God's plan to gather all his chosen ones into one flock is revealed.

Truly, our God has the heart of a shepherd for us. May the shepherds of his church today do likewise, empowered by the Spirit. And may we exhibit the heart of the Good Shepherd by caring for those the Lord has given us in our own little fold—whether it be in a family or a religious community, or some other grouping wherein we have been charged with the care of the sheep.

HUNGERING AND THIRSTING FOR SPIRITUAL FOOD

Seventeenth Sunday of the Year

1. 2 Kings 4:42-44
2. Ephesians 4:1-6
3. John 6:1-15

ELISHA is chiefly remembered as one of the great Old Testament miracle workers. On one occasion he fed a hundred people with only twenty loaves of bread. That story, of course, was a foreshadowing of a future, even greater miracle of its kind.

A small chapel on the shore of the Sea of Galilee now marks the spot where Jesus once fed a great crowd of people with five barley loaves and two fish. This miracle, the multiplication of food, has an important lesson in it for us. Just as the physical food fed thousands that day, so Jesus would feed the church with bread from heaven. He himself would become the Bread of Life for his people.

At the Last Supper, it was revealed that Jesus' own Body and Blood would become another kind of food that was spiritual in nature. The Body and Blood of Jesus was to be eaten by those who would believe in Jesus.

How strong does this food make Jesus' followers? Look at St. Paul. The letters he wrote from prison—he had been jailed for preaching the gospel—were free of self-pity, anger, or fear. Rather, they were filled with words of faith and hope and love. Paul was indeed being nourished and sustained by heavenly food.

He wrote, not about hardships to be endured, but about being worthy of one's vocation. To be a Christian means being charitable, unselfish, gentle, and patient. These virtues are the manifest fruit of all true believers. The strength to be such faithful ones for God comes from hungering and thirsting for him and allowing him to satisfy all our needs.

THE BREAD OF LIFE

Eighteenth Sunday of the Year

1. Exodus 16:2-4, 12-15
2. Ephesians 4:17, 20-24
3. John 6:24-35

FOLLOWING God is not always easy. He helped his people gain freedom from Egypt, but they also found themselves in the desert, hungry and thirsty. Moses was soon hearing a lot of complaints.

God responded quickly to the Israelites. He showered them

with quail and manna. The manna did not drop ready-sliced, from the skies; it was a product of a shrub that grows in the wilderness. Its sap oozes from holes made in its branches by insects, turns white on contact with the air, and then drops to the ground. This was the bread from heaven that is still gathered and eaten today.

We see here how God uses his creation in carrying out his plans. The manna was a symbol of an even greater kind of food that God would provide for his children. Our Christian tradition sees the manna as a sign of the New Testament food for Christians, the Body and Blood of Jesus, given to us in the Eucharist.

Jesus said, "I myself am the bread of life." Man does not live by earthly food alone, but by depending also on Jesus. Another kind of spiritual food is the Word of God. Those who eat it will learn how to walk on the path of life.

The Christian path to life is radically different from the world's reckless ways. Paul exhorts us to give up the old way of life and in its stead, put on a new humanity. Our new self, created in God's image, can be full of holiness and goodness.

If we partake in the heavenly food offered us, we will become increasingly like our heavenly Father and his Son.

WALKING WITH JESUS

Nineteenth Sunday of the Year

1. 1 Kings 19:4-8
2. Ephesians 4:30—5:2
3. John 6:41-51

ELIJAH was a great spiritual leader. Because of his uncompromising stance, the wicked King Ahab denounced him as the troubler of Israel. Queen Jezebel was more direct in her opinions. She purposed to kill him at all costs.

Even holy prophets can fear for their lives. Elijah fled into the wilderness. When he finally paused for rest, an angel of God provided food and water for him. In the strength of that "angel food cake" he walked forty days and forty nights until he reached Mount Horeb. There God came to Elijah and assigned him his next mission.

Paul was not met by an angel, but he did see the risen Lord as he traveled to Damascus one day. From that roadside encounter, the persecutor Saul was instantly converted to the great preacher

Paul. He preached, as a prisoner for the Lord, with joy and conviction to the church at Ephesus. He encouraged those who had met and received Christ into their lives to now walk in humility and love with him.

Jesus is God's gift to humanity, sent to free us from sin. In the power of the Holy Spirit, we can thus turn from our sinful ways and imitate God himself. We can love and forgive one another as Christ has loved and forgiven us. Let there be no bitterness or anger within those who walk with Jesus.

Jesus not only meets us, but he promises to be with us and walk with us until we meet again when he returns. He said, "I myself am the bread of life come down from heaven. If anyone eats this bread, he shall live forever. The bread that I will give is my flesh, for the life of the world." He promises us a life with him forever.

As the years pass, we come to realize that we are never really alone. Jesus is our fellow traveler on the road of life. He sustains us with bread from heaven, his Body and Blood, which is infinitely more nourishing to the spirit than even Elijah's angel food was to him.

Each of us walks with Jesus. He is our lifelong companion, always at our side. Whether he meets us in special encounters, or is simply traveling at our side, we are always blessed with his continual presence.

THE GIFT OF WISDOM

Twentieth Sunday of the Year

1. Proverbs 9:1-6
2. Ephesians 5:15-20
3. John 6:51-58

WISE SAYINGS or proverbs emerge from the keen observation of human nature and practical life experiences. In meditating on them, one can gain a bit of wisdom by learning from others' mistakes and following the advice that is given.

The Bible compares wisdom to a woman who built herself a big house with seven pillars. Having prepared a sumptuous banquet, she sent her maidservants to invite everyone to come to her house. The guests who responded to her invitation would thus be nourished with her food and drink. Wisdom would fill them up.

Paul too reminds us to walk as wise men and women. He

assumes we have access to divine wisdom that keeps us from living foolish and reckless lives. And he is right.

How we live expresses what we know and whom we follow. When we relate in love, with joy, and with grateful hearts to God, we demonstrate that we are comprehending God's heart and have some knowledge of what the Lord's will is. We are not foolish, choosing to live uncontrolled and selfish lives, but full of wisdom and God's Holy Spirit. The age we live in may be an evil one, but we can make the most of our time as followers of Christ.

Among Jesus' many astounding statements, one was his declaration that, "I myself am the living bread come down from heaven." Had he lost his mind? How can he give us his flesh to eat? Jesus went on to say that eating his flesh and drinking his blood was actually the only way to have life eternal.

Was this madness or wisdom? Nonsense or truth? The apostles did not understand, but they believed Jesus' words. Certainly our Christian tradition has always taught that these words are absolutely true. The bread he gives is his flesh for the life of the world.

No royal banquet ever prepared by human hands can compare with the feast of life that is ours to enjoy each time we receive Holy Communion. Wise believers know where to receive Jesus' life-giving presence and how to continue on in wisdom's way.

SECURITY IN GOD

Twenty-first Sunday of the Year

1. Joshua 24:1-2, 15-18
2. Ephesians 5:21-32
3. John 6:60-69

SECURITY is one hope that sustains us through life. We want the security of financial provision, physical protection, and relational fulfillment. Our history records the steps we have taken either to obtain or to hold on to such security. The irony, though, is that people and nations are willing to sacrifice or risk everything to insure that security.

Israel's ancestors worshiped strange gods up to the time of Abraham. With Abraham, though, God changed the course of the Israelites' history (and ours) by entering into a covenant with him. He promised the Israelites a land of blessing and that they would be his chosen people. This covenant was renewed at Mount Sinai with Moses, and again at Shechem with Joshua.

Israel was promised magnificent provision in the Promised Land and an everlasting, covenant relationship with the God of the universe. Yet to remain in covenant relationship with God, the Israelites did have to risk everything. They had to give up their tradition of serving pagan gods and serve the one almighty God instead. They had to love and obey God with all of their hearts and souls and minds.

That ancient covenant has been superseded and sealed by Jesus' sacrifice on the cross. A more intimate commitment to a people has come to us in the person of God's own Son. St. Paul sought to express this relationship or commitment God had entered into with us.

The mutual love between husband and wife represented, Paul said, the loving bond that exists between Christ and his church. Just as man and woman become one, so we become one with Christ. Just as a husband leads his family and cares lovingly for his wife, so Jesus is head of his mystical body, the church, and lays down his life for her.

The church can count on the unswerving fidelity of Christ. We are reassured of his presence whenever we partake in the life-giving food and drink he provides in the Eucharist. His flesh is food indeed, and his blood is drink indeed. Our security rests in what God has done for us through Jesus, and in all the ways Jesus reminds us that we can trust in him. Such security will never be taken away from us.

GOD'S WORD NEVER CHANGES
Twenty-second Sunday of the Year

1. Deuteronomy 4:1-2, 6-8
2. James 1:17-18, 21-22, 27
3. Mark 7:1-8, 14-15, 21-23

WITHOUT laws society cannot exist in an orderly fashion. Laws are not determined arbitrarily, but rather drawn up by legitimate authority for the purpose of maintaining and promoting the common good.

The Ten Commandments are an expansion of the most basic moral law: do good and avoid evil. Many religious laws in Jesus' day, however, were not explicitly part of God's Ten Commandments. They governed ceremonial and ritual behavior and were many times observed with fanatical exactitude.

Jesus openly attacked this legalistic obsession of the Pharisees. He challenged their views about the Sabbath and ritual cleanliness, emphasizing the importance of one's attitude of the heart and personal commitment to the Lord, rather than the external fulfillment of traditional precepts.

Out of a sinful person's heart come such things as fornication, theft, adultery, murder, and greed. Such actions will result in divine punishment even when the doers are externally upright and religious people.

When the scribes and Pharisees objected to Jesus' setting aside their laws of human tradition, he quoted from the book of Isaiah, "This people pays me lip service/but their heart is far from me." It is the inner attitude that counts before God.

God is the Father of Lights, St. James says. Unlike the sun and the moon which wax and wane, God remains constant. Human laws and human ways change, but God's laws and his invitation to salvation never do. He has given his children the marvelous gift of the gospel, and they should not just listen to it, but joyfully and deliberately live by it.

Many laws need periodic updating, for situations change as time goes on. Vatican II's call for the renewal of the church in the early 1960s was one important response to changing times. God's Spirit will continue to lead the church in bringing the saving message of Jesus to an ever-changing world.

GOD'S HEART OF COMPASSION

Twenty-third Sunday of the Year

1. Isaiah 35:4-7
2. James 2:1-5
3. Matthew 7:31-37

OUR world is basically a hurting world. No matter where we look, we see people suffering both in body and in spirit. We tend to distance ourselves from those who are disabled, or suffering, or in some way different from us. We prefer everything in nice, neat packages—a tidy world that we feel safe and secure in. But this, of course, ends up building walls which isolate us from our fellow human beings.

The exile of God's chosen people was a disheartening kind of existence. God, however, provided the voice of prophets who predicted happier and better times to come. The proclamation was made in even extravagant terms: the blind will see, the deaf hear, the lame leap like lambs, and the dumb speak.

How extraordinary a picture! God is so generous with his grace that it spills over onto the hurting, rejected, and disabled. He promised to restore these poor ones to health and joy.

St. James, in his epistle, rejected the actions of those who extended their hospitality to others based on their material wealth rather than based on their need. Those who are poor in the eyes of the world are the very ones God has promised spiritual riches to in the age to come. Those rich in faith are to be the heirs of God's kingdom.

God speaks to us using a variety of signs, but these have to be interpreted properly. Physical affliction, for example, was almost always considered a sign of God's anger against someone in ancient times. It was thought to be God's way of punishing the wicked. For us today, however, we see it more as indicative of the sinful world we live in—an alienation from God which Jesus came to destroy.

Jesus, of course, has always understood the heart of the human person, rich and poor alike. While passing through a pagan, and therefore particularly despised area, he healed one of the afflicted natives of the region who was deaf and had a speech impediment. Touching the man's ears and mouth he said, "Be opened." Instantly, the man was able to hear and also speak clearly.

We too, like Jesus, should care for those hurting in body or spirit in order to draw them closer to the Lord and his message. We must be willing to leave the security of our little world to share our faith with others.

COMFORT OR THE CROSS?

Twenty-fourth Sunday of the Year

1. Isaiah 50:5-9
2. James 2:14-18
3. Mark 8:27-35

WE LIVE in a world centered on and catering to self. Being good to ourselves seems always to be of the highest priority. Spas, health clubs, leisure centers, recreational parks, and entertainment are available everywhere. The goal is to feel good all the time. Relax, enjoy, be happy. If all else fails, try for instant happiness via alcohol, sex, or stimulants.

The alternative to all this is labeled "suffering." Nobody likes to suffer but it is part of the real world, even for God's people.

Isaiah the prophet spoke four times about a servant of God who was to suffer much more than any human being ever had or ever will. Through all persecution and affliction, he would not break down. His face would be set "like flint," confident that he would be vindicated in the end. He would even suffer to the point of death, but from his death new life would result for many.

This suffering servant had something that sustained him. His faith enabled him to suffer for the plans and purposes of God. Patience, endurance, and perseverance in trials are endured only through such faith in God. They are even called good works in the Bible, pleasing to God and admirable in the eyes of men and women.

Jesus our Savior did not flee from suffering. When Peter tried to dissuade his Master from going to Jerusalem to suffer and die, he was rebuked for not having the mind of God. There are times, then, when God's most beloved must endure great pain and affliction for his purposes to be fulfilled.

Jesus extended just such a startling invitation to his followers, "Deny [yourself], take up [your] cross, and follow in my steps." It is a call to live the life of the Spirit: "... but whoever loses his life for my sake and the gospel's will save it." It is a hard call, yet it is a call filled with grace. Jesus' own example proves this, and those who love God understand. They accept suffering, offer it up as a sacrifice of obedience, and walk with the Master. This is not the wisdom of the world, but wisdom that comes from God. Rather than the fleeting pleasures of this world we receive instead deep, heavenly, lasting joy and peace.

THE CALL TO SERVE

Twenty-fifth Sunday of the Year

1. Wisdom 2:12, 17-20
2. James 3:16—4:3
3. Mark 9:30-37

CHRISTIANS are called to a humble life of suffering and service. But how difficult it is to live this gospel ideal in our selfish and materialistic modern culture! We crave the popularity of a superstar and want to do the important things at home and at work. We try to avoid suffering at all cost and aim to lead a comfortable life.

Yet the Old Testament reading reminds us that we will invariably face strife, jealousy, and sufferings of all kinds if we take the Christian life seriously. Those who are not following God's ways will be particularly upset with us, because our Christian example will sting their consciences. But this is no reason to waver in our resolve to follow the Lord. Instead, it is all the more reason to seek his grace and help.

Further, the apostle James reminds us that a party spirit of contention and envy within the church herself is also a very real danger. We must counter this through a peaceful and docile spirit, instead of demanding our own way and getting into bitter disputes with our brothers and sisters in Christ. If we do give way to such a contentious spirit, James warns that that kind of attitude of heart is just the sort of thing that can lead to violence and even murder.

By contrast, Jesus identifies childlike, humble service as a mark of the kingdom of God. His chosen twelve had just been arguing over who was most important among them. So he sat them down and told them that the greatest is called to be the servant of all. Moreover, the greatest are called to be obedient and simple like children in God's kingdom.

Jesus, the greatest of all, reminds us that he is our model and inspiration in responding to this gospel ideal, for he willingly embraced death for our sake in obedience to his Father.

LOVE AND RESPECT FOR ALL

Twenty-sixth Sunday of the Year

1. Numbers 11:25-29
2. James 5:1-6
3. Mark 9:38-43, 45, 47-48

WE SEE someone who is different from us, and our eyebrows are raised in consternation. A young man's hair is too long, or a lady's dress seems out of style and out of place. We jump to conclusions, maybe even mistreating or disqualifying someone merely on the basis of appearance.

But God sees things quite differently. He sees the heart and pours out his Spirit on those who are ready to receive him. God rejects a ghetto mentality and reminds us that he doesn't play favorites.

In the Old Testament reading, Moses reprimands Joshua for just such a display of favoritism. The Lord had just poured out his Spirit on seventy of the elders among the Israelites when two men who had not been at the gathering received the Spirit as well. Joshua is upset and reports this to Moses, even asking Moses to stop the two.

Moses' response is telling. He asks Joshua if he is jealous for his (Moses') sake, and then states emphatically that he would like to see God's Spirit poured out on all the people! Moses is seeing with God's eyes of love and compassion for all, whereas Joshua is placing limits on God's action.

The apostle John also had to be corrected for tunnel vision. The disciples had just been given the authority to expel demons in Jesus' name when they encountered someone not of their company expelling demons in the Master's name. John tells Jesus that the disciples had tried to stop the man. But Jesus tells him no one who performs a miracle in his name can speak ill of him. The man should have been left alone by the disciples.

The message is clear. God's Spirit is not limited to those with whom we keep company. He is not even limited to denominational lines. Instead, God's Spirit is at work in all those who seek him with a sincere heart. May that be our attitude of heart when we encounter those who are different from us!

GOD'S ORIGINAL PURPOSE

Twenty-seventh Sunday of the Year

1. Genesis 2:18-24
2. Hebrews 2:9-11
3. Mark 10:2-16

BIBLE stories are in a class by themselves. They are visual stories— we see the action unfolding before our eyes. Today's story of the creation of man and woman is a good example of this. It is anthropomorphic, that is, God is portrayed in the story almost as if he were a man himself. God walks about in the garden, molds clay, breathes into it, makes a man. Then out of man's side, he makes a woman.

Man and woman were alike, of the same nature. They came from one body. From the very beginning, God intended man and woman for one another and the propagation of the human race. Hence, the integral connection between mutual love and procreation in marriage. Love brings forth new life!

Jesus was once confronted by Pharisees who tried to trap him in his speech. They asked him if divorce was wrong since Moses had allowed it. Jesus answered without hesitation, "Therefore let no man separate what God has joined." There shall be no divorce under the new Law of Love because its frustrates God's original intention for the human race. It was allowed by God under the old Law only because of the human race's sinfulness and separation from God.

Yet divorce is widely practiced today. After all, the logic goes, one has to be happy and free from being tied down by an imperfect partner. The Catholic church, however, remains clear on its stance, according to the teaching of Jesus. A valid marriage binds partners together until death.

What about annulments? The Church does sometimes grant annulments under certain circumstances. They are granted when it is established that the marriage in question has—because of some basic flaw in the contract—never been valid from the start and thus is not binding as a true marriage covenant.

The majority of people enter into marriage in good faith. Drawn by love, they pledge a lifetime commitment to their partner in a divinely established way of life. They know they can count on God's grace to accompany and help them in good times and in bad. Marriage can and will work out with God's help.

Jesus, the Second Adam, would bring many sons and daughters to glory, for by dying and fulfilling God's will, he becomes the perfect Savior responsible for the entry of human beings into the glory of God. A valid and healthy marriage reflects this kind of oneness, which was an important part of God's original plan in creating the human race.

WISDOM FROM GOD

Twenty-eighth Sunday of the Year

1. Wisdom 7:7-11
2. Hebrews 4:12-13
3. Mark 10:17-30

IN A PRAYER offered at Gideon, a holy place near Jerusalem, King Solomon began his reign by asking the Lord to help him be a good ruler. God heard his prayer and granted him the gift of wisdom—a gift of surpassing excellence.

Practical skills are both useful and necessary, but wisdom is the basis for perceiving what is ultimately important in life. It is seeing things through God's eyes and understanding them through God's mind. It plays a part in deciding how we are to lead our lives. It gives us God's priorities for this life.

The Word of God is like a sharp two-edged sword, cutting through confusion, darkness, or simply empty talk. God's *living* Word, that is, the gospel and the church's teachings, enters into play as we formulate our attitude toward life. We need both the Word of God and the wisdom of God.

A young man once came to Jesus, seeking direction as to how he might have a share in everlasting life. He was given a lesson in wisdom. Was he calling Jesus "good" because of the loving way he treated children? Did he really know the commandments?

Then the final test was put before him; he must renounce all to receive eternal life from God. Salvation is no easy matter, whether for the rich or for the poor. Family, friends, and earthly possessions are things that can keep one from seeking God. The young man did not like the wisdom he received from Jesus. Even the apostles were stunned by Jesus' words.

Jesus conceded that his proposal was comparable to a camel going through the eye of a needle, but explained that those who, for his sake, left behind all they held dear, would receive back a hundredfold now, and in the age to come, everlasting life.

Wisdom, partly gift and partly acquired through the Word of God, helps us choose the way of life that will best lead us to eternal life.

WILLING SERVICE

Twenty-ninth Sunday of the Year

1. Isaiah 53:10-11
2. Hebrews 4:14-16
3. Mark 10:35-45

WHEN dining out, a good waiter or waitress adds to the enjoyment of the occasion. Courteous clerks make shopping a pleasure, and a kind hospital staff heartens us when we are ill or afraid.

There is nothing demeaning about serving others. It is rather an honor and privilege, especially when one is a servant of the Most High God! Abraham, David, and the Blessed Virgin Mary gloried in their association with the Lord, and referred to themselves as his servants.

But being servants can come at a very high price. Those who serve nobility, for example, are expected to behave and act in a very exacting manner. Their actions are a direct reflection upon those whom they serve. The Servant of the Lord, as Isaiah described him, willingly endured suffering for the sins of others. A splendid crown of glory awaited him for his obedient and costly service.

Jesus serves us not only as a priest, but as the great high priest. Though perfect, he suffered temptation and is now capable of sympathizing with our weaknesses. Having suffered and died for our sins, he is now exalted at the right hand of God in glory. From on high, Jesus continues to serve us by helping us in our time of need.

Those called to leadership in the church—especially in this age of the laity—must be prepared to share Christ's life of service and of suffering. When James and John asked to rule with Jesus in glory, Jesus rejected their request. Leadership in the church is different from that of the world. By his atoning death, Jesus demonstrated just how different a leader in God's kingdom acts. A Christian leader serves and lays down his life for the church.

One of the many honorific titles given to the pope is that of Servant of the Servants of God (*Servous Servorum Dei*). It is a reminder that the preeminence of the pope is not due to his human endowments, but to the fact that he has been called to be like Christ himself. The Son of Man came not to be served, but to serve, and to give his life in ransom for many.

TURNING POINTS

Thirtieth Sunday of the Year

1. Jeremiah 31:7-9
2. Hebrews 5:1-6
3. Mark 10:46-52

THE PROPHET Jeremiah suffered a great deal in his lifetime. He foresaw Israel's sin and Yahweh's impending punishment of the people, only to suffer contempt and rejection by Israel's leaders. For this, he lamented both to the kings of his time as well as to the Lord himself. But he also brought a message of hope and restoration for God's broken nation. In fact, we owe to Jeremiah some of the most buoyant passages in the Bible.

In his proclamation of Israel's return to Zion we hear only of joyful celebration and the love of God for a fatherless child. The exile and the return of Israel are two turning points in the history of God's people.

The priests of ancient times were chosen by God to offer gifts as a sacrifice for their own sins and the sins of others. They have been replaced by Jesus, our sinless high priest, who is God's own Son. He is the eternal high priest of the order of Melchizedek. His coming, of course, is the ultimate turning point in the history of the world.

It is hard to see and appreciate such spiritual realities with our human eyes. Yet we want to see! We are like the blind man in the Gospel, begging beside the road. Through Jesus, our eyes have been opened! That day was a turning point in blind Bartimaeus' life. Our lives are changed forever, as well, when we gain spiritual sight to understand heavenly realities.

If we wish to see Jesus, we have to draw closer (other mature Christians will help us do this) and ask him for help that we might see him clearly. When we do receive new eyes to see, we can choose, as Bartimaeus did, to turn from our old ways and follow him who is the Light of the world.

THE GREAT COMMANDMENT

Thirty-first Sunday of the Year

1. Deuteronomy 6:2-6
2. Hebrews 7:23-28
3. Mark 12:28-34

NOT A DAY goes by without our thinking and talking of love. I love someone, somebody loves me. "Love makes the world go 'round," as the song says. It is the most basic and significant element in a person's life. Love is the breath of life. Without love there is little or nothing to strive and live for.

Contrary to what people may think, however, there is a right and a wrong way to love. A love that demands or is self-centered will wither away. It kills rather than brings life. Such love is not really love at all. The love of God and love for God that we read about in the Bible is a different kind.

In the famous passage in Deuteronomy, Moses said: "Hear, O Israel. The Lord is our God, the Lord alone. Therefore, you shall love the Lord your God with all your heart, and with all your soul, and with all your strength." As God has loved us, so we must now love him unselfishly and with all our being.

Declaring this to be the first and greatest commandment, Jesus linked with it another passage now familiar to all, "You shall love your neighbor as yourself." We naturally love ourselves, think of ourselves, and wish the best for ourselves. Now through God's grace, we are called to love, to think of, and to wish the best for others. This is not always easy or "natural," but it is spiritual and of God.

St. Paul reminds us of Jesus' supreme example of love. He understood Jesus to be a special, eternal priest. Unlike priests of old, he needed no sanctifying; he was holiness itself. He was also the perfect sacrificial lamb offered to God, once and for all time, for the remission of the sins of all humanity. How amazing is the love of God!

Our appropriate response is to thank God and to obey all his words. We want to love God and our neighbor. Through his grace, we can do so.

GENEROUS HEARTS

Thirty-second Sunday of the Year

1. 1 Kings 17:10-16
2. Hebrews 9:24-28
3. Mark 12:38-44

ONE day, a prophet in exile named Elijah saw a poor widow preparing a frugal meal. He asked her for water and bread. Poor as she was, the widow was willing to share what she had with him. Elijah promised her that the Lord would reward her generosity.

The poor we shall always have with us, Jesus said, and our soup kitchens and shelters bear witness to the truth of his words. Traditional works of charity were extolled in the book of Proverbs, "The kindly man will be blessed,/ for he gives of his sustenance to the poor" (Proverbs 22:9).

Charity, however, is more than merely sharing one's material goods. Each gift can speak the beautiful language that we call love. When we give freely, we give something from our hearts as well as the gift itself.

Judas objected to the waste involved when Mary poured out expensive ointment onto Jesus' feet. Jesus rebuked him, saying, "Leave her alone." He saw that the sweet ointment was in fact an expression of love based on the woman's spiritual intuition of his coming death and burial.

Jesus also approved of another widow's gift to God of two pennies. The two pennies could hardly buy much. But it wasn't the intrinsic value of the object that was important, rather it was the generosity it represented of the widow's heart. Are the poor to be denied the right and privilege of making a noble gesture, a loving act of sacrifice? Generosity is not the monopoly of the well-to-do.

Jesus himself, the great high priest, gave us an example of extraordinary generosity. He laid down his life for the sins of all humanity. He gave himself up, a perfect sacrifice, overcoming by that one single act the malice of the sins of all men and women.

Every Mass reminds us that love and sacrifice go together. And every Mass also reminds us that in giving, we receive abundant blessings from God in return.

THE END OF IT ALL

Thirty-third Sunday of the Year

1. Daniel 12:1-3
2. Hebrews 10:11-14, 18
3. Mark 13:24-32

WE COME, finally, to the end of the church year. The calendar year also approaches its end. All things, even the world as we know it, must end. It is time for serious thought on this fascinating subject.

The end of the world is immensely intriguing. How and when shall it come about? The Bible does not contain specific answers to such questions. It does speak of the end times in a very imaginative way.

These days we tend to think of the end in terms of nuclear bombs—a big bang followed by silence. The Bible views the end of the world primarily as the vindication of the just and the triumph of good over evil. The end will usher in the new era of happiness in God's eternal presence.

Michael the Archangel plays a role in this, for he has the title of Protector of the Church. We are reminded too that Jesus is always caring for us. He is our great high priest, who offered himself as the one perfect sacrifice for all sins. He is now with God in heaven where he prays for us.

Matthew, Mark, and Luke all speak of the end. Many others as well no doubt thought that the end was near. Not Jesus though. When he spoke of it, he referred to the exact timing as classified information. Only the Father knew the day and the hour. *That* was not among the things that Jesus had come to reveal.

The fall of Jerusalem was a cataclysmic event for some, comparable to the collapse of the cosmos. In speaking of this, though, Jesus had no intention of providing us with a blueprint of the future. He did tell us that goodness will triumph over evil. We certainly want to be on the victor's side when that final day comes!

A KING UNLIKE ANY OTHER

Christ the King

1. Daniel 7:13-14
2. Revelation 1:5-8
3. John 18:33-37

WE USUALLY associate kings with power and glory, even though the institution of kings is foreign to us today in America. A king was one who defended his people and defeated the enemy. He ruled his land and his people with love and justice. He took care of his subjects. He inspired his subjects to obey his laws and be loyal to him in good times and bad.

Yet Jesus of Nazareth had no armies and no kingdom. He conducted no campaigns for wealth, prestige, or power. But he has captured the minds and hearts of those who have come to know what he stands for. Jesus is, through no grasping or pursuit on his part, the King of Kings.

Daniel describes this humble king as the Son of Man who is given an everlasting dominion. In fact, Jesus called himself the Son of Man, pointing to himself as the fulfillment of Daniel's apocalyptic vision of the Son of Man's enthronement in heaven. Christian tradition has perceived the great truth in this, that Jesus was both God and Man. "Through him all things were made," and in him all creation shall once more be brought into unity.

No other king ever conquered sin and death. Jesus did so by dying and rising again. Eternal sovereignty was bestowed upon him by his heavenly Father, and all who follow him have become a royal priesthood—a people set apart by God to serve the King forever.

Pilate asked Jesus if he really was the King of the Jews, and Jesus explained that his kingdom was a spiritual kingdom. In this kingdom, his people would be defended and protected from sin and error by Jesus who is Truth himself.

Year C

Sunday Readings

ONE

Advent Season

WAITING WITH HOPE

First Sunday of Advent

1. Jeremiah 33:14-16
2. 1 Thessalonians 3:12—4:2
3. Luke 21:25-28, 34-36

WE ALL know how vexing it can be to wait for a phone call, a letter, an appointment, or the repairman. Sometimes the waiting is exciting—a baby is on the way, a loved one is coming home, or one's health is improving. Or maybe we are even in line for a raise!

The really exciting thing about waiting expectantly—also known as hope—is that it can extend to spiritual matters. Jeremiah touched on this when he stirred the people of Israel to hope in the coming of the Messiah. He called him the "just shoot" or "branch" who would inaugurate a glorious new era of justice and righteousness.

Promises are a source of life for us. They inject purpose and meaning into our daily lives. They make it possible for us to endure present trials and challenges as we look ahead to the reward or fulfillment of the promise.

The Thessalonians were eager to see the fulfillment of God's promises. Like us, they found it a challenge to wait over a long period of time. God expects us to use our time on earth getting ready for the big event. Like them, we sometimes fail to appreciate that life is part of the process toward the fulfillment of the times. The "not-yet" time is itself a gift from God. It is time to grow in faith and trust.

St. Paul urged the Thessalonians to "make still greater progress" in the kind of life they were living. To grow in love of God and neighbor is the most appropriate way to prepare for the Lord's coming.

147

The coming of Jesus at the end of time will be the climax of all creation. The evangelists did their best in trying to describe what will happen. They naturally drew heavily on their imaginations, using the time-honored figures of catastrophe—signs in the sun and the moon and the stars.

Ultimately, however, we must all wait on God. His is the world and all that is in it. The future of the world, and of all who are in it, is also in God's hands. While longing for his coming, we can live with a sure and certain hope that rests on the unfailing promises of God. Jesus' birth demonstrates that God follows through on even his wildest promises with those whom he loves.

PREPARE YOUR HEART

Second Sunday of Advent

1. Baruch 5:1-9
2. Philippians 1:4-6, 8-11
3. Luke 3:1-6

MANY people, once they leave home, find that "distance makes the heart grow fonder." They long for the familiarity of home. People forcibly ejected from their homes, or, worse still, driven into exile in a totally foreign land, dream of returning home one day.

The lot of the chosen people was exile and slavery. Any hope of change seemed impossible. Nothing is impossible with God, however, and he called on Baruch, a man of vision, to proclaim the glorious return of the Israelites to Jerusalem.

The rest is history. There was a return. Jerusalem, the city whose very name speaks of peace, became a symbol of God's people dwelling in peace, justice, and glory.

St. Paul learned, through a special grace, God had actually come down to earth in his Son, Jesus, to make his home among men and women. Paul also learned, to his astonishment, that there was to be a place for pagans in God's plan of salvation. He never tired of sharing this great revelation with others. Both Gentile and Jew alike would have the same heavenly Father and live in the same heavenly home one day for all eternity. The key, Paul stressed, was persevering right up until the day of the Lord's Second Coming, an important Advent theme. Then Christ would reap a rich harvest of souls upon his Second Coming.

In preparation for the Lord's first coming, John the Baptist summoned his listeners to be baptized as a sign of their turning from sin. Penance is not the most popular topic to preach on to others. John spoke so authoritatively and urgently that people began to wonder if perhaps he might not be the Messiah himself.

John was quick to disavow this; he was only a herald like Baruch, a voice crying in the wilderness. But his commitment and courage are lessons for us. Let us prepare our hearts for the coming of the Lord of glory at Christmas by turning away from sin.

## Looking to God	**1. Zephaniah 3:14-18**
Third Sunday of Advent	**2. Philippians 4:4-7**
	3. Luke 3:10-18

"Religion takes the joy out of life. People who take God seriously never have a good time." We know that some people stereotype Christians in this way, but the saints of God do not really fit into that picture. Quite the contrary, they are usually happy, confident, and productive.

There is much written these days about addiction to drugs, alcohol, sex, work, and even cleanliness. Enjoying good things can be overdone. Ill health, low self-esteem, shame, guilt, and alienation from God are all the results of compulsive or addictive behavior.

Thank goodness, though, that one wrong step does not lead us down an irrevocable path of destruction. We can get back on the right track. The prophet Zephaniah lived in terrible times, but he believed that there was hope for those who trusted in God for help and deliverance. On the Day of the Lord, God would show his justice, and perhaps more comfortably, his mercy. Ever ready to forgive, God offers sinners peace and joy when they return to him.

St. Paul echoes the prophet's sentiments. He assured his friends that if they prayed to God, he would reward them with a most extraordinary gift—an inner peace beyond anything they could imagine or comprehend.

We must look to God. If we do, we shall find ourselves sharing in his way of thinking and setting aside our narrow, selfish, futile ways. Jesus did not do what everybody else was doing. He shared his life with society's rejects and outcasts, tax collectors and sinners, soldiers and laborers, and drew them to himself.

John the Precursor used water to baptize repentant people. He who was to come, however, would use far more purifying agents. Jesus would baptize with the Holy Spirit and fire.

As we prepare for Jesus' coming—the Lord is near—we can remember that he will reward the fruitful lives of the saints. He will also punish wickedness and sin. The Lord will separate the chaff from the wheat at harvest time. Chaff will only be useful for burning at that time. So shall it be for the sins of men and women. Let us be without the chaff of sin as we welcome the Savior at his birth and look forward to his coming again.

WELCOMING JESUS WITH JOY

Fourth Sunday of Advent

1. Micah 5:1-4
2. Hebrews 10:5-10
3. Luke 1:39-45

PROPHECY is much like silk-screening. In the art form, one color is carefully applied after another, until the complete picture comes together, delighting the eye of the beholder. In prophecy, bits of information about a future person or event are introduced into a narrative. Since these items are introduced, initially in isolation, their meaning is not immediately grasped.

Micah's prophecy is quite clear, however. The Messiah was to be born where the glorious King David first saw the light of day. Bethlehem, about five miles south of Jerusalem, was situated in Judea. The king to come from that small town would be the very King of Peace.

We must not neglect the religious significance of prophecy. He who was to come would be one to do the will of God perfectly. His one perfect sacrifice would surpass and render unnecessary any other. Jesus offered his own body in sacrifice that we should thereby be made holy through him. This king's reign would extend across all physical territories. His kingdom would be an eternal, spiritual one.

St. Luke, in his Gospel, skillfully sets the stage for the coming of the Messiah. He describes a meeting between two expectant mothers, Elizabeth and Mary: the one old, the other young.

When these two mothers met, so did the sons in their wombs. John leaped with joy in Elizabeth's womb. The forerunner acknowledged the presence of the one announced. It was a moment full of meaning: the old covenant greeting the new.

Returning Mary's greeting, Elizabeth was filled with the Holy Spirit, and proclaimed Mary blessed. Mary was the mother of the one who had been foretold by the prophets, and was now here in the very home of Elizabeth.

As we approach Christmas, we can imitate Elizabeth who recognized and rejoiced in the first appearance of our great Lord and Savior, Jesus Christ. We can also be like Mary who was wholly committed to the Lord's will and obeyed his every word.

TWO

Christmas Season

For Christmas, see Year A, page 23.

MUCH FOOD FOR THOUGHT
Holy Family

1. Sirach 3:2-6, 12-14
2. Colossians 3:12-21
3. Luke 2:41-52

TODAY'S Gospel gives us much food for thought about family life. There is Mary and Joseph's understandable sorrow and concern over losing their twelve-year-old son, and then their astonishment on finding him talking with the elders and teachers in the temple three days later. What parent has not experienced dread and anxiety at losing their child? What parent has not also experienced astonishment and surprise when their child does something which seems to be completely out of character?

There is also Jesus' puzzling reply, "Did you not know I had to be in my Father's house?" Does this not speak eloquently of the need to place our relationship with God at the very heart of family life? Jesus was placing his relationship with God the Father above all other concerns. How easy it is today to let the busyness of work and family life crowd out prayer!

Further, there is Jesus' example of obedience. Even though his parents did not understand his actions, he returns to Nazareth and is subject to their authority. The challenge is for children to obey even when they feel they have been misunderstood.

Finally, there is the example of Mary treasuring this incident and other mysterious events in Jesus' life in her mother's heart. Is this not a perfect model of a mother holding dear to her heart the mysterious action of God in her child's life—straining to see God's purposes revealed and fulfilled?

Along the same general theme of family life, Paul stresses the mutual love, self-sacrifice, and respect that should characterize married life. He also points out the duty of children to obey their parents—a commandment that the child Jesus fulfilled perfectly.

Likewise, Sirach reminds us that our duty to our parents includes caring for them in their old age—even if their minds begin to fail. How relevant this message is today with so many living to a ripe old age and in need of care.

For Mary, Mother of God,
Second Sunday after Christmas,
and Epiphany, see Year A, pages 25, 26, & 27.

A MOMENTOUS STEP

The Baptism of the Lord

1. Isaiah 42:1-4, 6-7
2. Acts 10:34-38
3. Luke 3:15-16, 21-22

THE DAY a child takes his first step is an occasion for rejoicing. A beginning has been made, a new direction taken. A future full of promise and mystery lies ahead. Today we celebrate another kind of step. Jesus, a grown man, was baptized in the Jordan River by John the Baptist. In its own way, this was a first step of immense importance.

John was a precursor or the "forerunner"—one who went on ahead to announce the coming of an important personage. John was so impressive a figure that some of his hearers thought he was the long-awaited Messiah himself. John scoffed at the idea. He was only the herald and would become insignificant when the one announced appeared.

The Messiah would, John said, baptize with the Holy Spirit and fire. Fire is often associated with God in the Bible. It also is often connected to the Spirit. Who was this man, who could confer the divine Spirit on others?

As Jesus stood praying in the waters, the Holy Spirit descended upon him in visible form as a dove. A voice was heard from the heavens, "You are my beloved Son. On you my favor rests." The messianic era had begun. It was then that John the Baptist himself knew that this Jesus was the Messiah.

Baptism is the first step in our spiritual journey through life. Jesus' baptism was the beginning of his public ministry. It marked his decision to undertake the work of salvation. By being baptized like other human beings, he manifested his resolve to identify himself with sinners and to carry out the divine plan for salvation for the whole world.

Can this be of any possible relevance to us who live in the twentieth century? The answer of course is yes. Jesus is proof for us that God is no respecter of persons. Jesus came, identified with, and died for the people of every tribe and nation. It was in the house of a pagan, Cornelius, that St. Peter really saw this and rejoiced.

The church, faithful to its Lord, preaches the gospel to all nations and baptizes all believers so they can progress on their journey through life to God.

THREE

Ordinary Time before Lent

FRESH VISION OF GOD
Second Sunday of the Year

1. Isaiah 62:1-5
2. 1 Corinthians 12:4-11
3. John 2:1-12

ANY SOCIAL grouping, whether made up of doctors, artists, athletes, or members of a family, tends to develop its own special speech patterns. This is quite natural. Through constant usage, however, some words lose their zest and flavor. When this happens, we appreciate the poets and prophets among us who come up with new ways of expressing old words and phrases. They use words in fresh and unexpected ways to inspire and even startle us out of our routine ways of thinking.

When we are in love, endearing terms come naturally to our lips. Isaiah addressed his beloved city, Zion, with endearing terms too. Calling Jerusalem "My Delight" or "[My] Espoused" inspired others to see Zion in a new light. It awakened the longing to see Jerusalem restored, adorned like a bride for her husband. The Lord can speak so powerfully to us through his creative words in prophecy.

When you think of it, God does treat us as a tender, loving husband treats his wife. He is, for example, lavish with his gifts. St. Paul mentions many charismatic gifts (healing, prophecy, tongues) enjoyed by the church in Corinth. Human nature being what it is, however, Paul reminded his converts that God's gifts should not be the cause of ambition or pride. All gifts come from God and all have the same purpose: to edify and encourage the church.

At Cana, "the bashful water saw its God, and blushed!" wrote the poet, Cranshaw. What a beautiful turn of phrase, indeed, to describe Jesus' first public miracle. Jesus and his mother were both feasting at a wedding banquet when Mary's motherly eye noted a distressing fact—they were running out of wine. She brought this to Jesus' attention and then said to the waiters, "Do whatever he tells you." The jars freshly filled with water soon turned out to be the best wine of all.

This sign says many things about Jesus and God. One reminder is that God is concerned with even our most mundane domestic joys and sorrows. Signs and miracles are another way God creatively jolts us out of our ordinary way of thinking, so we can see his truths with fresh vision. Let us thank God today for his creative power to reveal more of himself to us.

RESTORATION AND REBUILDING
Third Sunday of the Year

1. Nehemiah 8:2-4, 5-6, 8-10
2. 1 Corinthians 12:12-30
3. Luke 1:1-4; 4:14-21

RETURNING from Exile, Israel faced two very urgent tasks. The walls of Jerusalem had to be rebuilt and the temple restored. Progress was slow until Ezra the priest and Nehemiah the governor appeared on the scene.

Both men had the wisdom to see that the Israelites needed *spiritual* restoration before any effective *physical* restoration could occur. Thus Ezra gathered the people to hear him read from the Book of the Law of the Lord. The people listened, received the Word of the Lord, and agreed to observe God's ways once again. Nehemiah then proclaimed a day for rejoicing and celebrating in the Lord. God's Word was being restored to its rightful place in the hearts of his chosen people.

In a letter to the Corinthians, Paul used an ancient comparison to explain the nature of the church. Just as in the body there are many parts, each important in its own way, but with only one head, so in the church there are many members, all vital, but with the one head, Christ.

The hand is not the eye or the foot; each member of the body has its own function. One part does not impede or render the others useless; they are interdependent. If one part hurts, all parts hurt. Honor paid to one is shared by the others. Concern for human dignity flows from this teaching. By honoring and building one another up, the church is strengthened and built up as a whole.

One Sabbath in Nazareth, Jesus went to the synagogue as was his custom. He stood and read from a passage in Isaiah. All eyes were upon him as he calmly announced, "Today this Scripture passage is fulfilled in your hearing," referring, of course, to himself.

Jesus did indeed bring glad tidings to the poor, release captives from their bondage to sin, and performed hundreds of miracles. Most importantly, he restored men and women to friendship with God.

In returning to God, we have spiritually restored our lives in him. Now we too can strengthen the city of God by doing our part to build up the church.

THE COURSE OF LOVE
Fourth Sunday of the Year

1. Jeremiah 1:4-5, 17-19
2. 1 Corinthians 12:31—13:13
3. Luke 4:21-30

LIFE is no fairy tale, no cruise on tranquil waters. It is a perilous adventure, a challenge at every step, a trip into the unknown. Perhaps this seemed especially so for some of God's great prophets.

This was certainly the case with young Jeremiah. Jeremiah heard the voice of God commissioning him, but he didn't like what he heard. He was told to undertake a task bristling with difficulties, and tried in vain to escape. Only the comfort and strength God promised Jeremiah prevented him from ignoring the call placed on his life.

What makes someone accept an unpleasant task? Love has this power. Jeremiah carried out his unpopular mission for forty years because of his love for God, and perhaps more importantly, God's love for him.

In perhaps his finest passage, St. Paul spoke at length about love. He personified love, saying that it is *patient* and *kind.* Love is not jealous, not snobbish, rude, or self-seeking. Love is always ready to forgive. Compared to love, no spiritual gift is important. Prophecies, tongues, and knowledge will one day cease, but love—never.

One day, in the Nazareth synagogue, Jesus declared before the public that he was the promised Messiah. He was already well-known for his miracles, but this was going too far. The people of Nazareth *knew* who he was! He was just the carpenter Joseph's son. But when Jesus announced that the good news was also for pagans, *that* was the last straw.

Dragged out of the synagogue, the religious leaders planned to throw Jesus over a cliff at the edge of the city. God protected Jesus, but he made his point. You will be persecuted for saying the truth, yet such suffering will be the mark of a true Christian.

We can pray that no matter what God calls us to do, we will obey and love him faithfully until the end.

THE VOICE OF GOD	1. Isaiah 6:1-2, 3-8
Fifth Sunday of the Year	2. 1 Corinthians 15:1-11
	3. Luke 5:1-11

VISIONARIES always attract followers, yet visions are unsettling things. One day the prophet Isaiah was praying in the temple at Jerusalem when he had a vision that was to change his life forever.

He saw the Lord seated in majesty, his long robe trailing down the steps of his throne. Attendant angels sang, "Holy, holy, holy Lord...." Isaiah then heard God say, "Whom shall we send?" Isaiah at once cried out, "Here I am, send me!" He had no idea what his task would be, but he was willing. With these words, Isaiah's illustrious career began.

While on his way to Damascus, St. Paul also heard the voice of God. It transformed him from persecutor to ardent missionary of Christ. Paul preached what he had heard: that Jesus had truly risen from the dead.

At that time, some were disputing the validity of the resurrection. But Paul resisted all attempts to water down or overspiritualize the gospel. Jesus had died for our sins and risen to new life. Paul made it clear that without Jesus' resurrection, the true faith is futile and empty.

In the Gospel of Luke, we see yet another example of the effect of God's call on an individual. At Jesus' word, the fisherman Peter set sail for deeper waters. He was a professional fisherman who had spent a fruitless night fishing, yet at Jesus' command he was ready to try again. The results, of course, were magnificent—fish enough to fill two boats!

The voice of God is compelling, and those who obey him are rewarded abundantly for their obedience and faith. Isaiah, Paul, and Peter all encountered the awesome voice of God. Although the power and call of God can be frightening at times, if we are willing to follow him and trust in his care for us, he will surely use us to accomplish his mission on earth.

Guided by the pope and the bishops, the church has carried on this mission throughout the ages for the salvation of all who would believe. We listen carefully for the voice of God so that we may respond wholeheartedly to whatever he wants to say to us.

WISDOM IN GOD

Sixth Sunday of the Year

1. Jeremiah 17:5-8
2. 1 Corinthians 15:12, 16-20
3. Luke 6:17-26

WE ARE justly proud of the technological expertise which we have shown to the world. Does, however, our ability to manipulate material things mean that we are wiser than ages past? The answer to that depends on what we mean by wisdom.

Ancient writers held wisdom in high esteem and took time to study and define it in hope of acquiring it more fully. Wisdom is much more than mere information; it involves having the proper orientation to life. Jeremiah said that a person who put his or her trust in material things was like a dry scrub in the wastelands. The person whose heart turns from the Lord is cursed.

But the one who places God first is like a tree planted near life-giving waters, able even in times of drought to bring forth fruit. A truly wise person draws strength from the inexhaustible spiritual source which we call faith.

Jesus' resurrection is the very heart of Christianity. For some the belief that Jesus rose from the dead, was seen by many, and is now seated at the right hand of God was simply foolishness. Not foolishness to Paul though. On the contrary, for him as for us, it is the unshakable foundation upon which our faith rests.

"If for this life only we have hoped in Christ, we are the most pitiable people of all," Paul wrote. Jesus is the firstfruits of those who have died. We look forward to our own resurrection and the life to come. It is wisdom for us to build our lives on this reality.

In the Sermon on the Mount, we see the difference, again, between what God values and what human beings do. To see things as the Lord does and to value the things he does is essential for obtaining wisdom.

Today's readings provide us with many examples of godly wisdom versus the world's foolishness. Without the Lord's help we would choose the blind or foolish path of human understanding. But in his mercy and love, he shows us the true, wise path of life through the Scriptures and the teachings of the church.

GROWING IN VIRTUE

Seventh Sunday of the Year

1. 1 Samuel 26:2, 7-9, 12-13, 22-23
2. 1 Corinthians 15:45-49
3. Luke 6:27-38

DAVID, the great hero of the Old Testament, had everything—looks, strength, and courage. He was a musician (harpist), song writer (wrote the Psalms), and poet. He was a valiant warrior and, most importantly, a man after God's own heart.

King Saul was so jealous of David that he sought to kill him. In the days that followed, David showed unusual compassion toward Saul. He refrained several times from slaying the king because he respected him as one of God's anointed.

This nobility of soul well befitted him from whose line the promised Messiah would come. Jesus, the Son of David, was more noble than David, wiser than Solomon, and a greater lawgiver than Moses himself.

Jesus told many stories that captivate our imagination. He painted vivid images about the coming kingdom of God. No armies were needed to establish and defend such a kingdom, because it was a spiritual kingdom. In it believing mortals would find the glorious things all people dream about: peace, justice, love, mercy, and forgiveness of sin.

Citizenship in this kingdom is obtained by baptism, a second birth that introduces us into a mysterious new, inner life. Through Jesus, each member of the kingdom is destined to grow in holiness, to advance in the heavenly way of life, and—imagine this!—to become perfect as our heavenly Father is perfect.

True disciples imitate their masters. Jesus commanded his followers to obey the law of love. He taught very specifically about generosity, forgiveness, and love of neighbor. Those who follow these directions become mature and holy people—fit company for David, Paul, and the rest of the saints who have gone before us.

SPEAKING AND LIVING FROM
THE HEART

Eighth Sunday of the Year

1. Sirach 27:4-7
2. 1 Corinthians 15:54-58
3. Luke 6:39-45

A VOICE reveals a great deal of information about the owner: one's sex, age, nationality, and often even a person's educational and geographical background. A person's voice also reveals his or her emotional state—whether the person is happy, sad, angry, afraid, and so on.

With this in mind, the Bible draws some wise conclusions. Big talk takes no brains and is not enough. Results are what count. It does no good to say, "Lord, Lord," when one's heart is far from God. Language can be a smoke screen hiding vicious thoughts that lead to sinful actions. We must listen carefully to what the heart is saying.

St. Paul was a man wholly centered on Jesus Christ. And why not? Who else in the history of the world had ever conquered sin and death, or risen from the tomb, and is now very much alive? Only Jesus. Paul urged his Corinthian converts to be steadfast in the work of the Lord, practicing their religion wholeheartedly.

Jesus spotted the shallowness of many who professed to be teachers of religion and spoke out strongly against them. They were supposed to instruct and uplift their pupils in matters of worship and morality, so as to bring them closer to God. But they were instead blind guides, ignorant of God's ways. Their guidance spelled only spiritual disaster and ruin.

How eagle-eyed we are when it comes to other people's sins or faults. How eagerly we point out how *they* can improve themselves. Jesus humorously (but in dead earnest) suggested that self-appointed critics should first tend to their own faults.

A tree is known by its fruit. Human beings are not trees, but the comparison is a good one. Words flow from what fills the heart, and our deeds speak more loudly about us than all our protestations of good will. We must see to it that we are good! We must speak and live from the heart.

AN ECUMENICAL SPIRIT

Ninth Sunday of the Year

1. 1 Kings 8:41-43
2. Galatians 1:1-2, 6-10
3. Luke 7:1-10

MANY many years ago, King Solomon built a magnificent temple for the Lord. Destroyed after several centuries, it was twice rebuilt. The second of these temples, the one Herod built, was the one Jesus prayed and preached in.

Solomon had prayed that his temple might be a place where even foreigners from distant lands might also come to pray and learn about Israel's God. He prayed that they might, along with the Lord's own people, respect the Lord and his holy temple.

Reading this ancient chronicle we are struck by the lack of exclusivity in Solomon's prayer. There is even the unconventional suggestion of allowing non-Jews to join in the worship of Israel's one true God.

The venture of ecumenism openly espoused by Vatican II will not fade away in our own time. It acknowledges a great theological fact. Many who are not of the fold, so to speak, can also be good Christians who follow God and are drawn to him in ways different from ours. We must respect others.

The centurion in today's gospel was a pagan who respected the Jews and their religion. He had even built a synagogue for them. He knew that Jews could not enter a pagan's house without becoming unclean, so he said to Jesus, "… I am not worthy to have you enter my house.… Just give the order.…"

Jesus was pleased with this man's faith and honor, so he instantly cured his sick servant. That centurion's profession of faith has since been incorporated into the liturgy as part of the Communion Rite.

Paul carried the good news to the pagan world and loved the Gentiles deeply, but he was angry with the Galatians when they tampered with the gospel's message. A truly ecumenical spirit does not mean watering down the truth of the gospel. It means speaking the truth in love. "Keep the faith" is still the bottom line.

FOUR

Lenten Season

For Ash Wednesday, see Year A, page 37.

SACRED TIMES

First Sunday of Lent

1. Deuteronomy 26:4-10
2. Romans 10:8-13
3. Luke 4:1-13

THE BIBLE often speaks of sacred times. Each spring, God's chosen people recalled how the Lord had "with his strong hand and outstretched arm" brought them out of the land of bondage into a land "flowing with milk and honey." At this time, the Jewish people presented the firstfruits of the land to the Lord as a thank offering.

Christians look on the day of baptism as a sacred time. Being baptized is the profession of faith we make which asserts that Jesus the Savior had died, but was then raised by God from the tomb, thereby breaking the power of death and sin forever. By virtue of this proclamation, the baptized share a new divine life in Christ.

The Gospels of Luke and Matthew both told the story of Jesus' temptation by the Devil in the desert. Although this episode manifested the wicked ways of Satan, it also magnified the purity and obedience of Jesus in contrast to the Evil One. Because of this, we as followers of Christ, now look back on those forty days as a source of inspiration. In its own way, it is another sacred period that we recognize, and are even in awe of, as a supreme example of Jesus' fortitude and holiness.

The enemy's attack reveals his cleverness, but also his weakness. Not even the highest of the fallen angels can enter a human heart unless it is invited in. The most the tempter can ever do is to suggest, "Go ahead. Do it."

Temptation is nothing but attractive bait dangled before us. We can always follow Jesus' example and resist it. No matter how attractive it may seem, the bait comes with a high price—the weakening or even the loss of God's friendship. Nothing is worth that. We can use even temptation as an opportunity to choose for God once again.

We can use even challenging times in our lives, as well as joyful and blessed times, as an opportunity to offer God a sacrifice of thanksgiving, praise, and obedience.

TRANSFIGURATION

Second Sunday of Lent

1. Genesis 15:5-12, 17-18
2. Philippians 3:1—4:1
3. Luke 9:28-36

WHAT would you think if, as I was speaking to you, I should suddenly begin to shine? You would probably look around to locate the floodlights. Jesus was transfigured on Mount Tabor, but there were no stage lights. The glow came from within.

The minds of the apostles must have raced furiously as they tried to comprehend this. What was happening before their eyes was not a disfiguration but a transfiguration, a change into divine splendor.

Theologians tell us that in Jesus Christ, two natures—one divine, the other human—existed side by side. Although these two natures resided in one person, neither one interfered with the other. To the outward eye, Jesus looked like anyone else, but there was certainly more to him than met the eye.

Splendor and glory and power are proper to the divine nature, but in Jesus they were under wraps, so to speak, so that he could carry out the task of redemption as a human being. Only this once, on Mount Tabor, was the glory allowed to manifest itself outwardly.

Why was it allowed? The transfiguration occurred to show the disciples in a striking way what lay ahead of them if they were to continue Jesus' work. Moses and Elijah were heard speaking with the Lord about his exodus or death. And in this somber context, a voice from heaven was heard saying, "This is my Son, my Chosen One. Listen to him."

The transfiguration of Christ was, then, a glimpse both into the nature of Christ and into the future. He who lived in the flesh would die on the cross for all humanity, and then be raised to everlasting glory with the Father. First the cross, then the crown.

The covenant God struck with Abraham, as with all God's covenants with humanity, are fulfilled and superseded by Jesus' life and death. Now we can look forward to being transfigured ourselves one day in heaven, even as he was on earth. Thanks be to God.

PHYSICAL AND SPIRITUAL REALITIES

Third Sunday of Lent

1. Exodus 3:1-8, 13-15
2. 1 Corinthians 10:1-6, 10-12
3. Luke 13:1-9

WHILE tending sheep near Mount Sinai one day, Moses saw a manifestation of the Lord in the form of a burning bush. When he drew closer to investigate he was ordered to halt and take off his shoes, for he was on "holy ground."

Moses was then commanded by the Lord to lead his people out of Egypt to a Promised Land flowing with milk and honey. Foreseeing that his authority would be questioned, he asked the voice in the bush, "What is [your] name?"

Semitic peoples have always considered names as something personal and not to be confided lightly to strangers. Knowing someone's name was almost like having power over him. The voice from the burning bush reflected this belief, for Moses was told, "I am who [I] am." It was a way of saying, "Mind your own business." All Moses had to do was what he was told. And he did just that. Some scholars also see in this divine name an indication of God's unlimited existence as opposed to the nothingness of the gods.

Many miracles attended the Israelite's exodus from Egypt: the presence of God in cloud and fire, the dividing of the Red Sea, manna from heaven, and water from the rock. The Christian pilgrimage parallels that of the Israelites: God's presence to us through the Holy Spirit, the waters of baptism signifying the passage from sin and bondage to freedom and life, the Eucharist as the true bread from heaven, and drink from the spiritual rock that is Christ.

God often uses physical happenings and manifestations to illustrate spiritual principles. From catastrophe and even violence, we learn the importance of always being ready for God. He is, to be sure, compassionate and patient, but God is also never to be tested or taken for granted. Like the owner of the fig tree, God patiently allows time for fruit to appear. But unless he eventually sees some signs of growth and change, he is capable of drastic action.

Lent is a time to reflect on the fruit of our lifestyle, to learn from our shortcomings and sins, and to do penance. We can grow in our awareness of God and of his teachings. We are always in his presence, and thus always on holy ground. We must respond as Moses did, in faith and obedience.

ELOQUENT ACTIONS	1. Joshua 5:9-12
Fourth Sunday of Lent	2. 2 Corinthians 5:17-21
	3. Luke 15:1-3, 11-32

THE RIVER Jordan, plunging headlong down toward the Dead Sea, once paused to allow Joshua and his people their crossing into the Promised Land. To remind future generations that God had helped his people do this, the Israelites erected a stone monument at Gilgal, and the Passover was celebrated for the first time.

Actions, then, can sometimes speak louder than words. Our attendance at Mass and our reception of the sacraments testifies to our awareness of how much we owe to God and how much we need him. We come to praise him. We thank him for his protection and help. He has brought us out of the desert of sin and into the Father's house.

St. Paul saw clearly that our restoration to God's good graces was brought about by Jesus. In him we are a *new creation*. Our life has only just begun. We are, now, as Paul says, the ambassadors of the good news about God. Our actions express the new hope and life we have in Christ.

The parable of the Prodigal Son is a gem of a story, perhaps the finest of the parables. Although a familiar and well-loved story, it seems always to be fresh and new. It also packs a solid punch, for when it ends, we are forced to ask ourselves the question, "Which one of the brothers am I?"

Leaving home, the headstrong younger brother squandered his inheritance and was soon destitute and disillusioned. Coming to his senses, he resolved to return home and acknowledge his foolishness to his father. He returned to a very pleasant surprise. His father welcomed his son back with open arms and was joyful and forgiving.

The elder son resented this, referring to his brother bitterly as "*your* [the father's] son." The father acknowledged the obedience of his eldest son over the years, but he pointed out that the prodigal son's return home was cause for gratitude and celebration. Like our heavenly Father, this father's mercy abounded beyond our frail, judgmental human nature. If you were the prodigal or the elder brother, how would you react? God's love is a continual challenge to all of us.

NEW HOPE WITH GOD

Fifth Sunday of Lent

1. Isaiah 43:16-21
2. Philippians 3:8-14
3. John 8:1-11

SOME people are pessimists, seeing only the dark side of things. Then there are the eternal optimists who are certain that everything is always going to turn out just fine.

Isaiah, the prophet, belonged to neither category. On the one hand, he was familiar with trouble. He remembered the story of his people's sojourn in Egypt and the oppression and bondage they suffered there. Imagine, then, how exultant Isaiah was when the Lord revealed his intention to do something new—something that would overshadow the great happenings of the past. That something would surpass even the miraculous Exodus from Egypt. We are speaking, of course, of the great return from the Babylonian captivity that would end the Jewish exile from Israel.

So it came to pass; and with it, a sinful race turned back to God. This same return happens to us, St. Paul said, when we believe and receive Jesus Christ. In the light of this surpassing knowledge, all earthly things fade into insignificance. Life on high with Jesus is a prize worth great effort.

Only eleven verses long, the story of the woman taken in adultery reveals to us how wonderful Jesus Christ is. One day the Pharisees brought before Jesus a sinful woman and put him on the spot. Should she be stoned to death, as Moses had prescribed, or not?

It was clearly a clever trap. Whichever way Jesus answered, his enemies could use his answer to make him look bad. Was Moses wrong? Were the Romans right in restricting the death penalty? As always, Jesus' reply bypassed the expected human tests to illustrate a more important spiritual truth. He said, "Let the man among you who has no sin be the first to cast a stone at her." Forced thus to face their own sins, these religious leaders began to slink away one by one from their judgment of the adulterous woman.

Jesus did not exonerate the woman of her sin, but he did show that there was mercy and justice for those who turn back to him. Let God judge these things, but do not you, he told the sinful woman, go on sinning. Sin is slavery and spiritual death. But through Jesus, God restores new life to all who have died through sin.

PALM SUNDAY

Passion Sunday

1. Isaiah 50:4-7
2. Philippians 2:6-11
3. Luke 22:14—23:56

PALM SUNDAY is a colorful pageant that marks the beginning of Holy Week each year. It contains all the elements necessary for a solemn celebration—crowds, a processional, the flourishing of palm branches, and shouts of joy and happiness.

Why all this excitement? It celebrates a great event that took place almost two thousand years ago: Jesus' entrance into Jerusalem was a decisive step to Calvary. This road eventually led through death to the resurrection. The Scriptures were being fulfilled. The whole world was to benefit from Jesus' death.

Church ceremonies are filled with symbolism. We are encouraged to explore the meaning behind the symbolism, especially during the last three days (or "*Triduum*") of Holy Week. Jesus' passion and death are the stunning revelation of God's love for his sinful children.

The prophet Isaiah spoke of a mysterious person he called the Servant of the Lord. Humble, reliable, and gifted of speech, this servant passed his master's teaching on to others. He was persecuted and rejected for this, but he held fast to the very end.

In a hymn about the incarnate Christ, St. Paul marvelled at Jesus' emptying himself of all majesty and honor proper to divinity. Jesus chose to become as human beings are—accepting death, even death on the cross.

Jesus' reward? God raised him on high and gave him the name above all other names. Jesus, the God-Man, is truly Lord. One day that will be acknowledged by the entire universe!

Jesus' march into Jerusalem was soon over. The palm branches were thrown aside, the shouting died down, and the crowds dispersed. But the final victory, the resurrection of Jesus Christ—the supreme revelation of God's surpassing love for sinners—will never be forgotten. Holy Week is a good time for remembrance.

*For Holy Thursday and Good Friday,
see Year A, pages 43 & 44.*

FIVE

Easter Season

For Easter Sunday, see Year A, page 47.

THE MYSTERIOUS WAYS OF GRACE
Second Sunday of Easter

1. Acts 5:12-16
2. Revelation 1:9-13, 17-19
3. John 20:19-31

IN TODAY'S readings, we see the unexplainable and sometimes mysterious actions of God. Yet through them all we receive his graces.

Solomon's Portico once ran inside Jerusalem's eastern wall, near the Golden Gate. After Jesus' resurrection, the apostles gathered there daily to preach the good news. Crowds of people came to hear their words and marveled at the signs and wonders that occurred. Some even placed the sick where Peter's shadow might fall upon them, believing that even that would bring about miraculous healings.

Miracles, a stumbling-block for many, are mysterious and marvelous events for which there is no human explanation. Miracles were an excellent way of getting people's attention before a sermon was preached, and St. Peter welcomed any chance to speak to listening ears about Jesus.

John, in exile on an isolated island, received a final revelation from Jesus. He was assured that Jesus, who had died, was now living and reigning forever—the holder of the keys of death and the nether world. For the next six Sundays, we shall be hearing from John's mystifying book. In all his visions, though, one thing is clear: good will ultimately triumph over evil.

Locked doors meant nothing to the risen Christ. Entering the room where the apostles were, he greeted them in his usual way, "Peace be with you." Then he breathed upon them the Holy Spirit and commissioned them to share the good news with others. He even endowed them with the power to forgive sins.

God alone can forgive sins, but he can do so through instruments of his choice. Miracles of grace come to us through his apostles and priests, and in secret ways known to God alone. Small wonder, then, that we still gather about the apostolic preachers, for we are certain that miracles of grace come to us through Mass and the sacraments.

THE AFTERMATH OF EASTER

Third Sunday of Easter

1. Acts 5:27-32, 40-41
2. Revelation 5:11-14
3. John 21:1-19

As NEWS of the resurrection raced through Jerusalem, the city was aroused to fever pitch. The apostles were brought before the Council of the Sanhedrin, given a stern talking to, and forbidden even to mention the name "Jesus." To help them remember this injunction, the apostles were whipped before being released.

"Better for us to obey God than men," the apostles retorted, as they resumed their preaching of the good news of the resurrection. The Beloved Disciple tells us that their brave witness to the Lord was echoed in heaven itself.

During his exile on Patmos, John the apostle saw in a vision an immense number of heavenly beings standing about the throne of the Lamb that was slain. They were singing his praises, for all honor, glory, and power is due him forever and ever. Indeed, this is the appropriate place for the risen Lord to be—worshiped and adored throughout eternity on his heavenly throne.

Shortly after the resurrection, the apostles had gone fishing, but without success. "Cast your net off to the starboard side," a voice from the shore advised. They did, and their nets were filled with fish. Jesus—it was he on shore—then invited them to eat the bread and the fish he had prepared.

The risen Christ comes unexpectedly to his friends—wherever they are, whatever they are doing. Needing nothing, he nevertheless says things like, "Bring some of the fish you just caught." He uses whatever we can offer him. Grace comes in and through what we have, wherever we are in his presence.

Another scene of great tenderness occurred after Jesus was resurrected and still on earth. Peter was given a threefold opportunity to profess his love for Christ (after denying Christ three times earlier) and then commissioned to "feed my sheep."

Jesus' last words to Peter were, "Follow me." Jesus is never far from his children. They have only to look up to see him, hear his loving voice, and rejoice in his risen glory.

NO EMPTY PROMISES

Fourth Sunday of Easter

1. Acts 13:14, 43-52
2. Revelation 7:9, 14-17
3. John 10:27-30

TELEVISION personalities who endorse products come on very strong in commercials, interrupting our programs with enthusiastic promises of happiness and contentment, if only we will buy their products. Their promises are, of course, empty ones; breakfast foods, cars, clothes, and smooth complexions do not bring happiness.

Happiness is the lure, to be sure, and religion has its sales people too. But what does Christianity promise? It promises trials and testings, rejection, and all too often, even persecution. But it also promises the assurance of life everlasting.

Who then would buy such a package? We do, as millions have over and over again throughout the history of Christianity. When Paul and his two cousins, Mark and Barnabas, brought the gospel to Crete and what is now modern-day Turkey, the Jews there rudely rejected them. This led to the decision to preach instead to the Gentiles. The Gentiles "were delighted… and responded to the word of the Lord with praise." Many Jews and Gentiles have, since the beginning of Christianity, received the gospel unto eternal life.

A prophecy was thus fulfilled. Israel's Messiah was, indeed, a "light to the nations." Even with persecution and revilement, the good news was so much brighter than the darkness of the ages. Thus converts have been won over to Christ all over the world throughout time.

John saw gathered about God's throne, in a vision, a crowd so huge that it could not be numbered. In it were those whose robes had been washed in the blood of the Lamb—a reference to the martyrs and all who had suffered for their faith on earth.

Jesus called himself the Good Shepherd. Sent by his heavenly Father, he would lead his sheep, not to visible pastures and springs, but to the waters of salvation. Small wonder that so many have listened to his voice despite hardship and opposition. Those who know his voice have tasted the goodness of the Lord and are assured that he not only promises, but delivers eternal joy and life forever more.

AN ASSURED HOPE

Fifth Sunday of Easter

1. Acts 14:21-27
2. Revelation 21:1-5
3. John 13:31-35

IF ALL the world were music, our hearts would often long for one sweet strain of silence to still the endless song. We are in the joyful season of Easter, yet we realize that our life on earth is like the weather, always changing. There will always be seasons of sadness as well as gladness.

When Paul and Barnabas revisited towns they had evangelized on their outward missionary journey, they said pretty much the same thing. Trials are inevitable, they told the elders. Those who enter the door of faith can expect good days and bad.

The cost of believing is high, but the promised rewards awaiting believers surpass imagining. John the apostle speaks about a new heaven and a new earth! Mourning and crying and pain will be no more. God is going to make all things new and will take up permanent residence in his new creation. At last there will be no more tears, trials, or death. This joyful kingdom will be glorious and unending.

Is this all a pipe dream? By no means. This hope is an assured one. Jesus' words to his disciples at the Last Supper instilled confidence in and encouraged them. More importantly, his words confirmed God's promises and prophetic message once the apostles looked back on what Jesus had said *after* he was raised from the dead. This became the unassailable basis for their hope in Christ and God the Father.

Jesus provided further comforts to his apostles for their time on earth before entering the glory of heaven. Peter the Rock would strengthen them, the Holy Spirit would empower them, and Jesus' own commandment would inspire them, "I give you a new commandment; love one another."

As we wait "in joyful hope" for Jesus to return and take us to his glorious heavenly home, we must show the world how much we support and love one another. Then whether the world is in good or bad times, they will see that we are living for another far better life to come. Though everything around us is unstable and changing, we remain fixed because of our eternal hope in Christ.

Renewal and Continuity

Sixth Sunday of Easter

1. Acts 15:1-2, 22-29
2. Revelation 21:10-14, 22-23
3. John 14:23-29

Today's motorists drive swiftly over superhighways with never a thought for all the time (sometimes years) and toil that went into their making. The church is like a giant superhighway, slowly taking form despite endless obstacles and the thousands of adaptations it must make to preserve and spread the gospel message to new times, places, and peoples.

One of the problems the early church had to face involved Jewish-Gentile relations. Was the new religion a variation of Judaism, or was it a completely new belief? This controversy led to the first General Council of the church, held in Jerusalem with representatives from as far as Antioch in attendance.

Their conclusion in writing stated: "It is the decision of the Holy Spirit, and ours, not to lay on you any burden..." (customs of circumcision, unclean food, etc.), which would impede social relations between Gentile Christians and Jews.

John's vision of the heavenly Jerusalem emphasizes the harmony, glory, and beauty that awaits all believers in heaven. There only the Lamb and the Lord God Almighty will be before us and in our thoughts. The frequent use of the number twelve suggests, too, a symbolic connection between the Old and the New Israel (twelve tribes, twelve apostles); again, we see the perfect harmony and wholeness between God and humanity.

At the Last Supper, Jesus foretold the divine indwelling of the

Father and the Son in the hearts of believers. He promised too that he would send the Holy Spirit to guide the church into the truth! As the times are being fulfilled according to God's schedule, an ever-deeper appreciation grows on the part of the church for the wonders and marvels of the divine plan that is unfolding before our very eyes.

New problems face the church in a constantly changing world. But we face the future confidently. The Holy Spirit is with us to strengthen and guide us along the way.

FORTY DAYS AFTER EASTER

Ascension Thursday

1. Acts 1:1-11
2. Ephesians 1:17-23
3. Luke 24:46-53

THE GREAT Doctor of the Church, St. Augustine, considered today's feast the greatest of them all, for it marked Jesus' entrance into a new and glorious condition of being.

The ascension took place near the Garden of Gethsemane, toward Bethany. After blessing his disciples, Jesus was carried up into heaven. The "up" is not primarily spatial; it essentially means that Jesus entered into God's presence. A cloud received him out of the apostles' sight.

Luke noted that forty days had passed since Easter. John, however, suggests that the resurrection and ascension took place simultaneously as Jesus rose from the dead. He did not have to wait for divine ratification. A formal and visible disappearance may well have occurred some weeks later.

The ascension does not imply that Jesus suddenly became inactive or disinterested in earthly affairs. Quite the contrary. Jesus sent the Holy Spirit from heaven to be with us as part of God's continual presence with us. Even now, Jesus is ever active, making constant intercession for us at the right hand of the Father.

Jesus did take a glorified human body with him into heaven. His body was both an instrument of our redemption, and a testimony to our worth. In heaven Jesus wears it still. When Jesus comes again, he will appear in that same glorified humanity.

The ascension filled the apostles with great joy, for they were now convinced that the Master was divine. Soon to be baptized in the Spirit, they would then begin their mission of carrying the good news to the whole world and initiating all nations into the mystery of faith through baptism in water.

The ascension had also, as Paul perceived, a cosmic dimension, for it spelled the overthrow of demonic powers. It was further proof that Jesus was ruler of all things and head over all.

St. Augustine was right. The feast of the ascension is a truly glorious feast, the crowning touch added to the death and resurrection of Jesus the Lord.

GOD'S HEROES

Seventh Sunday of Easter

1. Acts 7:55-60
2. Revelation 22:12-14, 16-17, 20
3. John 17:20-26

WE, as human beings, like and need heroes we can admire and imitate. The church thus honors the martyrs who have courageously given up their lives for the faith.

Stephen was the first of the martyrs. An able, quick-witted man, he was known for defending the new faith with great skill. His early success, though, resulted in his arrest on the grounds of blasphemy, a trial by the Sanhedrin, and death by stoning. Even in his death, however, he united himself with Christ as he prayed in words reminiscent of Jesus' own on the cross.

One of Stephen's persecutors was Saul, who soon became a Christian himself. A tireless and faithful apostle to the end, he also eventually died a martyr's death in far off Rome.

Jesus was the force or power that drove these men. John the apostle described him as the Alpha and the Omega. Risen from the dead, he is recognized now as the Beginning ("alpha") and the End ("omega") of all things. He stands triumphant in heaven, ready to welcome his faithful followers who have "washed their robes" clean in the blood of the Lamb.

How consoling to hear this mighty conqueror of death say to his disciples, among whom we number ourselves, "Come!" It is the invitation to share with him in his unending glory and to be intimately united with him who is the Morning Star shining brightly.

In his prayer at the end of the Last Supper, Jesus recommended the apostles to his heavenly Father, asking that he keep them close to himself. Through these apostles, the world would see something of the oneness between the Father and Jesus. They would learn of things more important than land, lineage, or language. They would see God's salvation through Jesus his Son. Among God's people, the world should see love, unity, and a blessed peace. God's heroes, saints, and martyrs have paved a path for us. Let us imitate them as they have courageously imitated Christ.

For Pentecost Sunday, see Year A, page 55.

SIX

Ordinary Time after Easter

THREE-IN-ONE

Trinity Sunday

1. Proverbs 8:22-31
2. Romans 5:1-5
3. John 16:12-15

MUSLIMS hold that there is no God but the one "Allah." The Jews are likewise monotheistic, believing in Yahweh alone. Belief in the divine Trinity is a distinctly Christian doctrine.

The Christian belief in a God who is "Three-in-One" is not simply a play on words. It does not require believers to swallow mathematical impossibilities as if 1=3 or 3=1. The Trinity surpasses human comprehension. Yet it is true.

We live most comfortably in a world that we can see, taste, or touch. The danger is that we can look on our tangible world as if it were the only kind of reality that exists.

Common sense tells us that there are invisible, immaterial realities. We cannot put love, friendship, truth, or justice on scales and weigh them. We cannot see or touch them. Yet these are precious realities, enriching the world. And God is more real than even these realities.

The Bible occasionally drops some hints about the nature of God. He is quoted as saying "Let *us* make man," or "Whom shall *we* send?" God is called *Elohim,* a plural noun, but always used with a singular verb. Such obscure details as these began to hold clear meaning when Jesus and the Holy Spirit came to God'speople.

We are, in such matters, like little fish swimming in a deep, mighty ocean. God is that ocean, sustaining, feeding, caring for, and loving us, insignificant as we are. In heaven, all the blessed

182 / Year C

shall rejoice in this sublime mystery of God. We believe in the Trinity—in three Persons with one divine nature.

THE GREATEST OF ALL GIFTS
The Body and Blood of Christ

1. Genesis 14:18-20
2. 1 Corinthians 11:23-26
3. Luke 9:11-17

ABRAHAM, returning from the rescue of his nephew Lot, was met by the priest-king of Salem, Melchizedek. He gave Abraham bread and wine and then blessed him. In return, Abraham shared with him some of the booty he had acquired.

This incident returns to us when we read about Jesus at the Last Supper. He too offered bread and wine. But he changed bread and wine into his own Body and Blood. This he gave to his disciples for their spiritual food and drink.

St. Paul assured the Corinthians that the tradition he had shared with them was authentic. Jesus had instructed his disciples to "do this, whenever you drink [my blood], in remembrance of me. Every time, then, you eat this bread and drink this cup, you proclaim the death of the Lord....

The apostles took him at his word. The Eucharist was more than a mere memorial of the Last Supper. It was Jesus' way to become personally present to them as their very own food and drink.

One day a crowd awaited Jesus, eager to hear him speak. Despite his fatigue, he preached to them about God and his kingdom. When it was time to eat, there were only five barley loaves and two fishes to feed a crowd of thousands.

It was enough, though. Through the apostles, Jesus distributed the loaves and fish until five thousand people were satisfied. Indeed twelve baskets were filled with the fragments that were left over! It was a miracle.

Jesus had a good reason for working such a miracle. It was one the apostles would not forget. It prepared them to accept his words at the Last Supper when he instituted the Holy Eucharist. Christians through the ages have, with their holy mother, the church, joyfully celebrated the greatest of all gifts—Jesus' own Body and Blood.

LIFE AND DEATH

Tenth Sunday of the Year

1. 1 Kings 17:17-24
2. Galatians 1:11-19
3. Luke 7:11-17

IS RELIGION just a waste of time? Far from it. Is it irrelevant to the issues of contemporary society? By no means. Religion is concerned with the cosmic struggle between good and evil, and with the powers of life and death.

After rebuking King Ahab for encouraging paganism in his land, the prophet Elijah fled the country; kings do not take kindly to open criticism of their policies.

Elijah found shelter in the house of a poor widow. When her only son died, the prophet breathed into him and restored him to life. The widow told Elijah she now knew that he was a man of God. The restoration of life can only come from God. No one else can defy death.

Centuries later, St. Paul wrote to the Galatians concerning the spiritual life. As a Pharisee, he had actively persecuted Christians. Through divine intervention he became Paul the Apostle and spent the rest of his life telling people about Christ. He was the primary preacher of the gospel to the Gentile world.

After spending three prayerful years in the desert, Paul had gone to Jerusalem to confer with the apostles and Peter. Paul's preaching, then, was sanctioned by the pillars of the church. His teachings came from solid, traditional roots. Believers should not run after novelties.

At Nain, a tiny village across the plain from Nazareth, Jesus performed an unsolicited miracle. Again a widow was involved. Her only son had died and was being carried to the cemetery. Telling the mother not to cry, Jesus stopped the procession and ordered, "Young man, I bid you get up." He did. Jesus displayed once again that God has power over life and death.

Christianity alone destroys the power of death and answers the questions that lead to physical and spiritual life.

GRACE AND LOVE

Eleventh Sunday of the Year

1. 2 Samuel 12:7-10, 13
2. Galatians 2:16, 19-21
3. Luke 7:36—8:3

THE BIBLE is a brutally honest book. It deals with sins of every kind, recording the havoc sin wreaks in human lives. Friendship with the king did not deter Nathan the prophet from denouncing David's adulterous affair with Bathsheba and the resultant murder of her husband. Such flagrant immorality demanded punishment and the Bible records that it was meted out.

In his sharpest letter, St. Paul rebuked the Galatians for tampering with his teaching about Christ, faith, and the law. Our friendship with God was not restored by observing the ancient precepts of the law, but through Jesus, who was sent into this world to save it. Men and women are justified by faith in Christ.

Paul makes clear that we are made pleasing to God by a gift of grace which begets faith. Although both grace and faith must be present, it is the gift of grace from God which enables us to have faith. The initiative is always God's. The response, however, is ours. The results are, as Paul wrote, "... the life I now live is not my own; Christ is living within me."

One day, when Jesus reclined at table in the house of a Pharisee, a woman with a bad reputation came into the room and began to wet his feet with her tears. She kissed his feet and wiped the tears with her hair. She then anointed them with ointment. Everything she did was a visual penance, a prayer for pardon. Her heart was where it ought to be, and she was forgiven. Jesus' calm acceptance of this shady woman upset his hosts. They could not see beyond the externals to her penitent heart.

Two debtors, Jesus responded, were absolved of their debts, one small, the other large. Which of the two would be most grateful and contrite? The one who was cleared of the larger sum, of course. So, too, was this woman's sins forgiven. Her great love for the forgiving one was an acceptable and pleasing sacrifice. Love, not sin, always has the last word.

SPIRITUAL DISCOVERIES

Twelfth Sunday of the Year

1. Zechariah 12:10-11
2. Galatians 3:26-29
3. Luke 9:18-24

GETTING an education is not easy. It requires a great deal of time, energy, talents, and resources. Yet nothing is more natural than our desire to acquire knowledge and understanding. God has put in us a thirst to know and explain what we see in this life.

There is, likewise, the wonderful world of the spirit. Many exciting and impressive discoveries await the explorer there.

In this new world, one learns about Jesus Christ, the Son of God, to whom we are united in baptism. By prayer, meditation, and Scripture reading, we learn how much God has loved us. We look intently upon him who was pierced and begin to see the reality of many marvelous spiritual truths.

Our physical world is governed by inexorable laws of nature. The spiritual world features something nature cannot explain or bring about. Today's reading in Galatians, for example, reveals that men and women from every race, culture, and background experience a spiritual unity that rests upon and witnesses to their common faith in Christ. Compared to this unity, that of the United Nations is nothing.

The world has never seen anyone like Jesus. He was a most unusual man. People attempted to explain and understand him, but with little success. Was he Elijah or one of the prophets? Even the apostles were slow to comprehend. Peter was the first to recognize Jesus as the Messiah.

There is always more to learn about Jesus and his teaching. Spiritual truths revealed by him require spiritual eyes if we are to receive them. The words, "… whoever loses his life for my sake will save it," are words of eternal life and have inspired generations of people to lead holy lives. He reminds us that there is another better world we may discover and even live in now. We need only ask the Lord for the eyes to see such spiritual realities.

THE COST OF DISCIPLESHIP

Thirteenth Sunday of the Year

1. 1 Kings 19:16, 19-21
2. Galatians 5:1, 13-18
3. Luke 9:51-62

LEADERS with charisma and vision draw followers to themselves from every stratum of society. Elijah, wearing the distinctive cloak of the prophet, one day came upon Elisha, who was busy plowing his land. The mantle thrown over Elisha's shoulders meant that he was to take the place of the great Elijah. The farmer Elisha became the disciple of Elijah the prophet.

Jesus, a man of crowds, was usually seen in the company of his twelve apostles. In turn, through these apostles, thousands of others would hear the Master's teachings. In this way, the church of God was born.

It was clear that Jesus intended to establish a church, for he said so in so many words. His followers learned that the cost of discipleship was high, yet still they came. His vision and promises of new life have never lost their power to challenge and draw men and women unto himself.

From a cell in a Nazi prison camp, Dietrich Bonhoeffer, a Lutheran pastor, wrote, "When Christ calls a man, he also bids him come and die." He was, of course, not speaking of physical death alone, but also of a death to self and to the ways of the world. Yet this death results in true, glorious life in Christ.

There is an urgency to Jesus' words. The choice cannot be put off. Once the hand is laid to the plough, there can be no turning back. "Let the [spiritually] dead bury their dead;..." Christ is either all or nothing for you.

Jesus the Savior cannot be appreciated without acknowledging the reality of human sinfulness. His words about sin sound severe and uncompromising, yet the break from slavery to sin is essential to true freedom. Such bondage should not be accepted. Each moment is important. Entry into the kingdom of God depends upon this important choice of casting off sin and receiving forgiveness from Christ.

By his own death, Jesus brought freedom to the world. His followers show their loyalty to him by faithfully putting the love of God and neighbor into practice in obedience to his words. That is not too high a price to pay for the privilege of being his disciples.

THE BELIEVER'S PEACE
Fourteenth Sunday of the Year

1. Isaiah 66:10-14
2. Galatians 6:14-18
3. Luke 10:1-12, 17-20

THE BIBLE frequently speaks of peace. For God's chosen people, living in slavery for four hundred years, peace must have seemed an impossible dream. Yet the day eventually came when the promised freedom became a reality. The Word of God through his prophets was vindicated. What was never promised anyone, however, was a life free from cares.

St. Paul, often faced with difficult situations, maintained an astonishing serenity of mind. In Christ he had become a "new creature," concerned only with the things of Christ. He took pride in the marks persecution had left on his body. Christ meant everything to him; the world meant nothing. The Lord Jesus Christ was all-sufficient. No wonder all the cares and strife he encountered in the world did not disturb his peace in God. Such talk sounds strange indeed to our materialist way of thinking. But those who know the friendship of God understand.

One of the most surprising things about God is that he has chosen to use ordinary people to accomplish his work on earth. He sent the Twelve out to preach the coming of God's kingdom, instructing them that nothing else was to take precedence over this task.

Sent out like lambs among wolves, the disciples soon learned how powerful they really were. Demons fled at the mention of Jesus' name. Jesus made it clear to his disciples, however, that the most important thing was that their names were written in heaven.

A rich crop calls for many hands. In every age, Jesus has chosen and sent out men and women out to preach the good news by the way they lived. In return, he promises spiritual peace and prosperity, freedom from the tyranny of the world and sin, and a greater love for the Father and his Son. This is the life for which we were created.

CHRIST-LIKE CONSCIENCES
Fifteenth Sunday of the Year

1. Deuteronomy 30:10-14
2. Colossians 1:15-20
3. Luke 10:25-37

MOSES loved and cherished God's law, and he urged the people to obey it. They did not have to climb mountains or cross the seas to find it, Moses said. It was near to them, even in their hearts.

Moses' words can be understood as referring, not only to God's written law, but also to that quiet, inner voice we call our conscience. By it we constantly decide on the right or wrong of things.

We must not act against our conscience, but the fact is that even our consciences can err in knowing what is right or wrong. At times we act impulsively or confidently without bothering to develop a formed conscience in Christ.

Learning that some of his converts were listening to strange teachings, Paul clarified the facts of the faith for the Colossians. Jesus is our unique, all-powerful Redeemer—truly God, yet also truly human. In him all things were made and brought back into unity. By his death on the cross, peace between God and humanity was restored. The church is Christ's body; he is the head.

Jesus' two great commandments were that we love God and love our neighbor. When asked who our neighbor is, Jesus told the story of the Good Samaritan.

Hearing this parable, people began to feel uncomfortable as they got the point. With which of the actors in the parable were they to identify? Jesus was not dealing with theory. He was forcing his hearers to examine their consciences in a practical way. He was forming their consciences in the ways of God.

Jesus wants us to be like the Good Samaritan, recognizing and meeting another's need no matter what the person seems like or what race he or she belongs to. The parable is clearly a call to shape our consciences in Christ. Christian faith and love must always be our guiding principles in life.

HOSPITALITY

Sixteenth Sunday of the Year

1. Genesis 18:1-10
2. Colossians 1:24-28
3. Luke 10:38-42

WHEN we offer hospitality, the Lord calls us to be gracious hosts, attentive to the needs of our guests. But even more importantly, he calls us to be open to each guest as a person, showing a personal interest and concern for the individual.

God manifests himself to Abraham by sending three men, probably angels, to visit him. Recognizing the divine visitation, Abraham hastens to prepare a sumptuous repast for his mysterious heavenly visitors. His gracious hospitality is rewarded when, after the meal, one of his guests tells him that about this time next year his wife Sarah will have a son.

The Lord Jesus himself is invited to dine with Mary and Martha. When Jesus comes, Martha is busy with all the details of the meal. But Mary is content to sit at the Lord's feet and listen to him. When Martha objects, Jesus tells her that Mary has chosen the better portion.

On one level, the Lord is explaining that our primary focus should always be seeking him and being attentive to his voice. We should not allow the mundane details of daily life to crowd him out. On another level, he is explaining that whenever we show hospitality or care for others, a personal concern for the person takes priority over practical details.

Ever the gracious host, God himself, Paul tells us, has condescended to reveal to us the mystery of salvation. As the Gentiles, we were once cut off from God, but now he has graciously drawn near by sending us Christ.

THE VALUE OF PRAYER

Seventeenth Sunday of the Year

1. Genesis 18:20-32
2. Colossians 2:12-14
3. Luke 11:1-13

LEARNING of God's resolve to destroy the people of Sodom for their sins, Abraham, the friend of God, began with surprising audacity to bargain with him. Should the many have to suffer for the sins of the few? He suggested alternate solutions to the Lord, and the Lord listened!

Abraham obviously believed that a loving and merciful Lord listens to the prayers of his friends. The power of intercessory prayer is indeed great. People hunting for jobs sometimes ask friends with good connections to put in a good word for them with their employers. They know that requests made by such friends can be a deciding factor in the hiring process.

By being baptized, St. Paul wrote, the Colossians had become God's special friends. Immersion in the waters of baptism symbolized their burial with Christ. Rising, coming out of those waters as Christ did from the tomb, they had become alive in a new and wonderful way. Freed from sin, they now live "with Christ" in God. Once united with Christ, we may be confident that God hears our every prayer.

The Gospels often noted that Jesus prayed. Impressed by this, the disciples one day asked him how they should pray. Through the Lord's Prayer, Jesus taught them the importance and effectiveness of persistence in prayer.

Prayer keeps us close to God. "Ask and you will receive;..."

promised Jesus. God, who knows all things, does not need to be informed about our needs. But it is good to express our dependency upon him. He who gives us many things without our asking will at other times give us things only if we ask him.

Prayer, however, is not magic. It is not a way of controlling God or bending him to our wishes. Jesus did not assure us that our every request will be answered the way we wish. Parents sometimes close their ears to children's demands. For a child's horizons are limited, and a no can in fact be the best possible answer. God's no is always a loving answer.

Abraham, Paul, Jesus, Mary, and the saints are all good examples for us. May no day pass without filling it with your prayers.

TRUE RICHES
Eighteenth Sunday of the Year

1. Ecclesiastes 1:2; 2:21-23
2. Colossians 3:1-5, 9-11
3. Luke 12:13-21

CENTURIES ago, a wise man called Qoheleth remarked upon observing all the toil and sweat of man's labor in this life, "Vanity of vanities, all things are vanity!"

Qoheleth was not condemning anybody for working hard. He was rather emphasizing that a person ought to keep his or her priorities straight. Security and planning for the future are legitimate human concerns, but they should not be the ultimate purpose for our existence.

The number of millionaires and billionaires in the world today makes Croesus or Midas look like amateurs. Greed is everywhere. As St. Paul says, the love of money is the root of all evil.

Traditionally, it was thought that goodness was rewarded with earthly success and prosperity; whereas, only the wicked would encounter bad luck and misfortune. We know, however, that many a scoundrel enjoys material wealth and saints can go hungry. In the end, though, those with money and possessions will realize there is much more to life than mammon. Yet those spiritual treasures will have evaded their grasp.

St. Paul urged his readers to raise their sights above earth to think of higher things. Vices attractive to the old self should not be entertained by those who have been resurrected to a new life.

We must all strive to grow in the knowledge of Christ.

Jesus once told a parable about a rich man whose one ambition in life was to grow richer. Living a self-centered life, unconcerned about others or their needs, this man died in spiritual poverty. All the wealth, which he had dedicated his life to acquiring, could not save him in the end.

Jesus' advice is still sound, "Grow rich in the sight of God." Look upon earthly things as blessings from God, but not as the greatest treasures in this life. Avoid selfishness, avarice, and greed. God is our richest possession.

JOURNEY OF THE FAITHFUL

Nineteenth Sunday of the Year

1. Wisdom 18:6-9
2. Hebrews 11:1-2, 8-19
3. Luke 12:32-48

THE BOOK of Wisdom tells us about life and how it should be lived. Every life has dark moments, but the darkness is never final. Nor does God need light to accomplish his purposes. Even darkness can be used by God to lead his people through life.

Paul's letter to the Hebrews was written to bolster up the faith and courage of converts from Judaism. He reminded them of the patriarchs Abraham, Isaac, and Jacob that God had raised up as leaders of his people. They had believed the Lord's promises and their faith was rewarded. Their trust in God gave them the faith perspective that helped them survive the crises they faced in their journey through life.

Earthly trials are part of God's plan. With his help, difficulties can be endured and overcome. The indispensable virtue in such times, however, is patience.

Some two thousand years after the patriarchs, Jesus came to dwell in the midst of his people. Even when Jesus was on earth with his disciples in human form, trials were ever present. Many were a preparation for the magnificent revelations Jesus was to make concerning life in the kingdom of God.

More than once, Jesus said, "Fear not!" to his disciples. He would not have given such an encouragement if there were no cause for his disciples to fear. Yet he exhorted them to continue to trust in God, to wait expectantly for the Second Coming, and to be faithful in good works in the meantime.

God has literally showered blessings upon all of us, but our journey through life with him still calls for persevering faith and expectant hope. We must be ready to meet the Lord anytime, anywhere, as his good and pleasing servants. We have been given much, but to whom much has been given, much will be required.

INSPIRING PEOPLE

Twentieth Sunday of the Year

1. Jeremiah 38:4-6, 8-10
2. Hebrews 12:1-4
3. Luke 12:49-53

TEMPERS flare when things go wrong. In 587 B.C., Jerusalem was besieged by the Babylonians. To make matters worse, the prophet Jeremiah declared that all this was happening as divine punishment for Israel's sins.

To silence the prophet, Israel's leaders lowered Jeremiah into a muddy cistern for solitary confinement. Cisterns were reservoirs for water that fell during the rainy season, but Jeremiah's cistern was only full of mud at the time. Jeremiah was lucky to get out of the cistern alive.

God's people need courage and determination, for they encounter trials of many kinds. Yet God has provided supportive friends—those whom Paul called "a cloud of witnesses." We can gain comfort and strength from the examples of those saints of old who have gone before us. Jesus himself was the perfect example.

In our fight against sin, we must not grow despondent or abandon the struggle. The third reading today examines Jesus' own pain while on the earth. He once cried out, "I have come to light a fire on the earth. How I wish the blaze were ignited!" This fire was the purifying action of God over the earth. His next words were also enlightening, "I have a baptism to receive. What anguish I feel till it is over."

Jesus linked this baptism with his death. This had to precede the kindling of spiritual fire upon earth. The shadow of the cross hung heavy over him not simply because he did not want to die, but more importantly because he longed to see God's full action upon earth unleashed. Even though Jesus was sinless, perfect before God and humanity, he suffered anguish on behalf of God's desires for the human race.

Jeremiah in his cistern, Paul's disheartened converts, and even the Savior himself, all knew agonizing moments. God's Word records these stories so we may take heart and be strengthened.

PURIFIED THROUGH SUFFERING

Twenty-first Sunday of the Year

1. Isaiah 66:18-21
2. Hebrews 12:5-7, 11-13
3. Luke 13:22-30

TODAY we hear Isaiah, Paul, and Luke speaking. What do they have to say to us who now live so many centuries after them?

The prophet Isaiah learned in a dream that the Lord was going to end Israel's exile. He would lead peoples of all nations to Jerusalem. Both Israel and Gentile converts would come to the temple, bearing gifts on clean vessels in worship.

This prophecy becomes meaningful for us when we understand that Jerusalem stands for the heavenly city of God. All nations will have come to the church. God is not limited to any one place or time, but can be found everywhere by all who seek him. Those who are purified in this life have a glorious inheritance awaiting them in heaven.

We do not need St. Paul to tell us about the trials of life; everybody has personal experience with them! But why does God permit such things?

The building of God's kingdom is not a spectator sport. It involves serious human sacrifice and endeavor. Ups and downs are not signs that God is angry with us. They are, in fact, the result of having a free will and the ability to make our own personal decisions. Through our choices and decisions, we grow in maturity and wisdom. In coping with our problems, we learn the value of discipline and purification. It is a very important lesson.

Suffering is part of our training. Unpleasant as it is, it bears fruit in peace and goodness for those who accept it. Take heart then. Gold is not harmed, but purified in the crucible. Jesus' disciples will enter in by "the narrow door." Awaiting them there, though, is a glorious place at the heavenly banquet table.

TRUE HUMILITY

Twenty-second Sunday of the Year

1. Sirach 3:17-18, 20, 28-29
2. Hebrews 12:18-19, 22-24
3. Luke 14:1, 7-14

HUMILITY is a character quality that is very hard to sell. Few find it attractive. It is certainly not extolled by the world. You never hear about it on television, or see positive portrayals of it in the movies or papers.

The Bible, however, praises humility as a virtue. God is pleased with the humble. He gives them grace as a sign of his blessing. The fact is that humble people are the salt of the earth.

The word "humble" means having one's feet on the ground, or being in contact with reality. Humility is related to honesty too; the humble person does not have to deny his strengths or talents. He simply acknowledges where those strengths and talents came from. They are gifts from God. Humble people should want to make good use of their gifts.

Jesus hated hypocrisy. Once at a banquet, he told a parable about humility. Those who push themselves forward, he concluded, will be humbled by God. Those who are humble in this life, will be the first in the kingdom of God.

The old covenant was sealed on Mount Sinai amid thunder, lightning, and a loud voice. The new covenant between God and humanity was sealed in blood on Mount Calvary outside Jerusalem. The earthly city symbolized the heavenly Jerusalem filled with choirs of angels and saints. It also prefigured the church in which each one is a "firstborn" and a citizen of heaven.

This heavenly homecoming is reserved for the humble. It is reserved for those who praise God for the good things that have come to them through Jesus Christ. True humility acknowledges the source of all goodness and gives credit where credit is due.

WISE MEN AND WOMEN OF GOD

Twenty-third Sunday of the Year

1. Wisdom 9:13-18
2. Philemon 9-10, 12-17
3. Luke 14:25-33

SOLOMON once made a pilgrimage to the high place of Gideon and asked the Lord for divine guidance. To lead an ordinary life in this world is perplexing enough, but to be king over God's people required serious help from on high. Solomon prayed earnestly for wisdom to lead God's people. Because of his seeking God, Solomon's reign marked the golden age of his people, and he became the wisest man on earth. God is not stingy with his gifts.

St. Paul was also a very wise man. He once baptized a fellow prisoner named Onesimus, a runaway slave. Although Paul loved Onesimus and counted him as his own child, he sent him back to his former master, Philemon, as the responsible thing to do. Paul, however, also urged Philemon to show mercy and blessing to Onesimus, even as Paul had blessed Philemon in the past. Like God the Father, Paul loved both parties, yet required of each of them righteous conduct toward one another.

Jesus, the only human being on earth who was wiser even than Solomon, came to set up the kingdom of God upon earth. He made it plain that entrance into his kingdom would not be an easy matter. One would have to learn to hate everything else in comparison to love of the heavenly kingdom.

To emphasize the cost of discipleship, Jesus told a parable about a man who was about to build a house, and another about a king whose territory was about to be invaded.

A person ought first to make sure that he or she can finish the job before starting to build a house. Likewise, to defend a kingdom, a king has to decide first of all if he can do so successfully. If not, he should sue for peace instead! Counting the cost of any decision is prudent and wise.

In order to be Jesus' disciples, we must count the cost as truly wise men and women of God. There is no other way to come to the Father.

THE MERCY OF GOD

Twenty-fourth Sunday of the Year

1. Exodus 32:7-11, 13-14
2. 1 Timothy 1:12-17
3. Luke 15:1-32

As Moses spoke with God on top of Mount Sinai, the people below busied themselves in making and worshiping a golden calf. This was a pagan symbol of strength and fertility. The Lord was outraged by this and would have destroyed the idolaters had not Moses intervened.

Moses reminded the Lord of his investment in this people. The Lord had performed many wonders on their behalf and had also promised their patriarchs a blessing on their descendants. The Lord honored Moses' plea on behalf of the Israelites and stayed his avenging hand.

Mercy is one of the most endearing things about God. Divine justice is tempered with divine mercy, said St. Paul. Because of God's mercy, Saul had been changed from blasphemer to believer. Did it not show God's patience and resolve to save sinners that he had revealed himself to the greatest sinner of all, Paul? To the Lord God be honor and glory forever.

The story of the prodigal son perhaps illustrates the mercy of God most eloquently. This young lad, inheritance in hand, left home for a fling in far-off places. Soon penniless, hungry, and lonely, this prodigal came to his senses and headed for home.

When the father saw his son returning home, he welcomed him with open arms. He cut short the boy's confession and gave orders for a big celebration. Great was the rejoicing in that household. The son who was dead had come back to life. He was lost and now was found.

Many a sinner since that day has been moved to come to his senses and return home. The welcome mat is always out at God's house. We need only to return and God will overwhelm us with his love and tender mercies.

THE CALL TO SOCIAL JUSTICE

Twenty-fifth Sunday of the Year

1. Amos 8:4-7
2. 1 Timothy 2:1-8
3. Luke 16:1-13

RESPECT for persons and property is essential if there is to be social justice in society. On one hand, this entails respect for and trustworthiness in handling the resources of another—this is essentially the social compact between all employers and their employees. On the other hand, employers must respect the rights and dignity of those in their employ, and society at large must safeguard the rights of its members—especially the poor and marginalized of society.

Amos of Tekoa, one of the minor prophets, is the most well-known prophet of social justice. He rails against the wealthy and powerful of Israel who are exploiting the poor through shady business practices and even outright dishonesty and cheating. The prophet warns these evildoers that God sees their crimes and will not forget how the poor and needy have been trampled upon.

In the Gospel, Jesus reminds us that if we are trustworthy stewards of the resources given us, we will be entrusted with more. Such trustworthiness, in matters both material and spiritual, starts with little things. Then we can be entrusted with greater things. An example is that of an employer—say a grocery store manager—who hires a sixteen-year-old boy as a bagger. The teenager is industrious and exemplary in his job, so he is promoted to the position of clerk and eventually that of assistant manager of the entire store.

Paul the Apostle reminds us that we should pray for our politicians and those in authority that they be honest and trustworthy. We should especially pray that they will value and uphold norms of social justice—particularly for those who are most marginalized in our society. God will not look kindly upon us if we trample upon the legitimate needs of the poor and needy!

DAY OF RECKONING

Twenty-sixth Sunday of the Year

1. Amos 6:1, 4-7
2. 1 Timothy 6:11-16
3. Luke 16:19-31

THE PROPHETS of Israel were troublesome people. They were not afraid to tell kings and important people that right was right and wrong was wrong. They were the conscience of Israel. Their obedience to speaking God's "hard truths" brought punishment and persecution.

Amos denounced in scathing terms the extravagances of the rich. He scorned their headboards inlaid with ivory, their tables groaning under fancy foods and choice wines, and their idle complacency in the midst of it all. Meanwhile, the poor went hungry. The day was coming, Amos thundered, when a bitter price would be exacted for such living. Their judgment would be captivity and exile.

God has always chosen men and women to speak on his behalf.

From prison, St. Paul twice wrote to his convert, Timothy, exhorting him to do God's work and to grow in faith, patience, love, and kindness. He was to "fight the good fight" until the Lord would come again.

Jesus had no equal as a storyteller. When he finished his parables, his listeners were often startled to discover that they themselves were part of the story. The parables were not about real people, but Jesus used types to impart spiritual truths for all who had ears to hear. Thus Dives is any proud, rich man, and Lazarus is anyone whom God has helped. Both men died, one going to Abraham's bosom, and the other to the abode of the dead.

True to his selfish nature, Dives wanted Lazarus to fetch him a drop of water. An impassable abyss, however, prevented this. Then Dives asked only that Lazarus alert his brothers to their danger of ending up in hell as well. Perhaps he feared they would add to his own torments there by blaming him for his bad example.

The requests were denied. Jesus said if the wicked would not listen to Moses and the prophets, then neither would they listen to one even raised from the dead. Jesus wanted to emphasize personal accountability. God's children are all responsible people. No matter what their state in life, each person must one day answer before God for the way he or she has lived.

WE LIVE BY FAITH

Twenty-seventh Sunday of the Year

1. Habakkuk 1:2-3; 2:2-4
2. 2 Timothy 1:6-8, 13-14
3. Luke 17:5-10

HABAKKUK is the strange name of one of the twelve minor prophets. He contributed three chapters to the Bible. Two of them contain a dialogue with the Lord, and the third a psalm of exceptional beauty.

Habakkuk's world seemed to be falling apart. He received a vision of mighty armies massing to attack the nation of Israel. God's people would be stricken and banished from their lands. Could it be possible, though, the prophet wondered, that these armies were instruments of the Lord and his justice to turn his people back to him?

The Lord commanded Habakkuk, "Write down the vision/

clearly upon the tablets,/ so that one can read it readily." The words were to reassure the people of God that truth and justice would, in the end, prevail. "...the just man, because of his faith, shall live."

Faith here means to hope and trust in God. A good person who is not overcome when beset by evil, will not only survive, but be rewarded. The Lord will see to it.

St. Paul lived in a different world than Habakkuk. Jesus had fulfilled all that was positive in the old law. Those who believed in Christ risen from the dead were now exempt from performing the works prescribed by the Law of Moses. Their righteousness comes from faith in what Jesus has done.

From a Roman jail, Paul sought to encourage Timothy in his faith. No matter how weak Timothy felt, or how much he was surrounded by false teachers of the law, he did have faith and love in Christ Jesus. These realities would sustain and empower him.

Jesus often looked for faith both in those who came to him for help and in his disciples. He taught that faith holds great power even when it comes in a form as tiny as a mustard seed. Trusting in his words and in his help, God's servants have always been able to do heroic, even impossible things.

Jesus, Paul, and Habakkuk agree on the importance of faith in God. With faith, we can be effective and pleasing servants of the Lord.

SPIRITUAL HEALTH

Twenty-eighth Sunday of the Year

1. 2 Kings 5:14-17
2. 2 Timothy 2:8-13
3. Luke 17:11-19

MEDICINE has made great advances in controlling and treating disease. Despite our best efforts, however, some illnesses (for example, leprosy, malaria, cancer) still defy our attempts to eliminate them. And we all know of the terrible sickness of AIDS, which scientists have yet to find a cure for.

In ancient times, illness was thought to be the work of evil spirits. People were quick to seek help from those who were thought to have power over evil forces. Naaman the Syrian, for example, went to Israel to be cured of leprosy by the holy man Elisha. Told to wash in the Jordan, Naaman did so and was cured. From that moment on, Naaman acknowledged the only one true God, the God of Israel. At first, though, he questioned the prophet's judgment. Naaman received the blessing of healing and belief in the one true God only after he finally obeyed God's prophet.

Sin is like spiritual leprosy. Sin alienates a man from God as effectively as leprosy used to isolate its victims from social contact. Unlike leprosy, though, sin can be rejected or chosen. The consequences of sin are not merely physical death, but a spiritual death that extends beyond life on this earth.

Some people who heard the good news refused to believe. They rejected Jesus' teaching and example. They also persecuted those who preached and lived the gospel. Despite such opposition, though, Christianity has never lost its power to convict and convert. As St. Paul said to Timothy, "... there is no chaining the word of God!" It continues to make its blessed way, against all odds, through the centuries.

Elisha and Moses cured single lepers. Jesus cured ten of them at one time. The one Samaritan sought out Jesus to thank him, but the nine others who were Jews did not. Jesus was disappointed in their lack of gratitude.

Gratitude is acknowledgment of a gift given and should be proportional to the gift itself. Jesus' gift to us is spiritual health and eternal life. Once we realize this, we should begin to say our thanks.

Do we live in gratitude to God as Naaman and the Samaritan leper did? Or are we like one of the nine? May God help us to live each day thankful and praising him for the spiritual health and healing from sin that he has given us in Jesus Christ.

PERSEVERING PRAYER	1. Exodus 17:8-13
Twenty-ninth Sunday of the Year	2. 2 Timothy 3:14—4:2
	3. Luke 18:1-8

As THE Israelites journeyed from Egypt to the Promised Land, they found the way blocked by the Amalekites. A fierce struggle ensued.

Moses, the Israelite's leader, took up a position where he could see how the battle was going. As long he held his arms outstretched, holding in them the staff of God, the Amalekites were driven back. When through fatigue he lowered his arms, the enemy gained control. Noticing this, Aaron and Hur seized Moses' arms and held them up. As a team they were able to gain victory over the Amalekites. Preachers have often used this story to illustrate the power of prayer.

Jesus provided the apostles with a good example of a prayer warrior. He prayed a great deal, and he often spoke about prayer. One of his parables features a poor woman bereft of her husband and in desperate straits. Her persistent demands for justice finally moved a corrupt judge to see that her needs were met. How much more, Jesus argued, will persistent prayer be answered by God.

Persistence is always a good thing, especially in the matter of prayer. It indicates faith and trust in God. It demonstrates one's confidence that God is not indifferent to his children's needs. Rather, he is good and will reward those who earnestly seek him.

We are blessed today in having a good modern translation of the Bible. As St. Paul says, Scripture is useful in many ways. It teaches us about God, corrects our errors, instructs us in right living, and reproves us for our sins. Thus it keeps us close to the Lord. One of the Bible's favorite topics is the faithful praying of believers.

PRAYING TO A JUST GOD

Thirtieth Sunday of the Year

1. Sirach 35:12-14, 16-18
2. 2 Timothy 4:6-8, 16-18
3. Luke 18:9-14

THERE IS hardly a man, woman, or child alive who has not at one time or other cried out, "That makes me so mad!" This explosion is usually prompted by some injustice done.

Law courts exist to settle conflicting claims, courts of appeals allow a thorough ventilating of disputes. Still, there persist many painful problems for which there seems to be no human remedy. What can one do in such cases?

The Bible says we can pray. The prayer of the just person pierces the heavens to where God dwells. He is always approachable and always on the side of justice and righteousness.

Prayer is an admission of the existence of a supreme authority,

God, who is sovereign over all men and women. Paul ended up in jail many times, always unjustly, and his response was always to pray.

True prayer is the cutting edge of a faith that is exercised in good times and in bad. It involves praise and adoration and an acknowledgment of God as God. Our prayers of petition in hard times are not displeasing to him, provided they are not self-serving. A humble prayer always ends with, "Your will be done."

Paul was confident that God would reward him as a faithful, praying man who had "… fought the good fight… run the race to the end… and kept the faith." He knew he could count on the Lord to keep him safe and bring him safely home.

Jesus described two men at prayer. The first one lectured God, reminding him how good a servant he was. The other man, a tax collector, acknowledged that he was a sinner and humbly asked God to be merciful to him. His prayer was the acceptable one to God. It is this man who went home justified.

MERCY AND JUSTICE	1. Wisdom 11:22—12:1
Thirty-first Sunday of the Year	2. 2 Thessalonians 1:11—2:2
	3. Luke 19:1-10

THE BIBLE has taught generations of believers that God is loving, patient, and merciful to all.

This idea is not new, but it is rarely presented so powerfully, serenely, or logically as in today's verses from the book of Wisdom. Kind and merciful, the Lord has not turned from what he has made. He is ever concerned about all his creation.

St. Paul's early converts knew that the Lord Jesus was going to return and that he would settle all accounts with mercy and justice. Some of his listeners thought this was going to happen tomorrow and began to watch the skies, neglecting their work. Jesus would indeed come again, Paul exhorted, but in the meantime, they should continue growing in holiness, living out their faith day by day.

Zaccheus was the chief toll collector of Jericho, the crossroads city not far from the Dead Sea. One day, hearing noise, he climbed a tree to see what was going on. Jesus was in town! Jesus called out to him, "Zaccheus, hurry down. I mean to stay at your house today."

One can imagine Zaccheus' amazement. This man knew his name and wanted to dine with him. Zaccheus responded to Jesus' visitation. He promised to give his property to the poor and to make good whatever he had taken unjustly in the past as a tax collector. He chose the new life offered him in Christ. Only Jesus' presence made this possible.

Jesus is always present to us. If we respond to him as wholeheartedly as Zaccheus did, we will be ready to receive justice as well as mercy when he comes again.

LIFE AFTER DEATH?

Thirty-second Sunday of the Year

1. 2 Maccabees 7:1-2, 9-14
2. 2 Thessalonians 2:16—3:5
3. Luke 20:27-38

CHILDREN often ask their parents, "Where did I come from?" As we grow older, we begin to ask another question, "Where am I going?" and "what will happen to me when I die?"

Some feel that we came from nothing, that we are a mere spark in the dark, soon to be extinguished as if we had never been. This answer leaves us sad and disappointed. Surely more can be said of life than that?

The Bible takes life after death seriously. In today's reading from the Old Testament, we hear of the seven heroic Maccabean brothers who died professing their belief that another life awaited them after death.

Those who die in the Lord know that after this life, they shall be with God in heaven. A full and joyful life is the splendid destiny God has in store for his children.

This conviction of a future life with God is a great source of strength and hope for Christians. St. Paul prayed that the Thessalonians would open their hearts and minds to this truth as they lived patient and faithful lives for God.

The Sadducees of old did not believe in the resurrection of the body. They challenged Jesus about this, hoping to show the absurdity of such a belief. Following the Levirate law laid down by Moses, a woman married seven brothers in succession. Whose wife would she then be after the resurrection? they asked.

Jesus destroyed their attack stating how different life after death would be from life on earth. After death there shall be no marriage or remarriage. God has provided something better for the next life. After the resurrection, we shall be wholly consumed with God himself. We shall see Eternal Truth, Beauty, and Goodness face to face. What a life to look forward to!

THE DAY OF THE LORD

Thirty-third Sunday of the Year

1. Malachi 3:19-20
2. 2 Thessalonians 3:7-12
3. Luke 21:5-19

THE PROPHETS often spoke of a *Dies Irae,* a "Doomsday," complete with fire, fearsome heavenly happenings, and a divine judgment. Malachi, last of the minor prophets, saw this as God's answer to the superficial, religious practice of the day.

Elijah, he prophesied, would come to announce this Day of Judgment. Jesus taught that Elijah had already come in the person of John the Baptist. He too spoke of that Final Day at length.

The end of the world was part of Christian teaching from the beginning. Paul preached it to the Thessalonians. They were so impressed by it that they stopped working to watch the skies for Jesus' return. Paul had to write another letter to straighten them out. Many other things had to happen first, he wrote.

"Master, look at those stones!" the disciples said to Jesus. They were looking at the huge blocks of stone which Herod the Great had used in updating the Jerusalem temple.

Jesus' reaction caught his disciples by surprise; "… the day will come when not one stone will be left on another." Was he speaking about the end of the world or about another fall of the city of Jerusalem? The language, apocalyptic in tone, is obscure, picturesque, and fraught with hidden meaning.

History tells of the fall of Jerusalem in A.D. 70, and of a second fall in A.D. 135. Both events were catastrophes of such magnitude that they could not be described by using ordinary terms. Both were also signs of an even more awesome future event to come—the end of the world.

Natural calamities are symbolic of spiritual trials. The disciples of the Lord will indeed know persecution, hatred, and betrayal. With God's help, though, our faith will grow stronger and we believe that one day we will see God's kingdom reigning forever.

THE GREATEST KING OF ALL

Christ the King

1. 2 Samuel 5:1-3
2. Colossians 1:12-20
3. Luke 23:35-43

KING DAVID ruled for seven years in Hebron and thirty-three more in Jerusalem. Those were days of glory. Solomon succeeded his father as king and further enhanced the glory.

Jesus was hailed as the Son of David. He worked miracles and was followed for a time by crowds looking for a leader who would restore Jewish independence by defying the hated Roman government. Jesus refused that role. He spoke consistently instead about spiritual freedom and a heavenly kingdom. The crowds rejected him. In the end he was crucified in between two thieves.

Oddly enough, the sign nailed over his head proclaimed him to be King of the Jews. Only on the cross did he in fact speak as a king. He promised paradise to the repentant thief on the cross next to him. From the cross he gave another truly regal gift to John the Apostle, entrusting to him the care of his Blessed Mother.

Earthly kings sit upon thrones, crowns on their heads and scepters in their hands. Earthly kings in the past dispensed justice, framed national policies, and took steps to insure peaceful existence for their people. One felt safe and cared for when a good king ruled.

We pay honor and homage today to Jesus our King. He is the Beginning, the first-born from the dead and the head of his body, the church. He, in whom perfect divinity resides, has made peace for us with God through the blood of the cross. Through him we have been saved from the power of darkness and sin and brought into the kingdom of everlasting light.

Jesus has done greater things for us than any earthly king ever did for his people. As members of his spiritual kingdom, we recognize humbly how much has been done for us. Brought into life by divine power and invited to share in everlasting glory, we will partake in the King's royal plan for his subjects. Our King deserves all our thanks and praise.